Praying for Reform

See www.lutheranvoices.com

LUTHERAN
VOICES

Praying for Reform

Martin Luther, Prayer, and the Christian Life

William R. Russell

Augsburg Fortress

Minneapolis

PRAYING FOR REFORM
Martin Luther, Prayer, and the Christian Life

Large-quantity purchases or custom editions of these books are available at a discount from the publisher. For more information, contact the sales department at Augsburg Fortress, Publishers, 1-800-328-4648, or write to: Sales Director, Augsburg Fortress, Publishers, P.O. Box 1209, Minneapolis, MN 55440-1209.

Editor: Scott Tunseth

Cover Design: © Koechel Peterson and Associates, Inc., Minneapolis, Minn.
          www.koechelpeterson.com

Cover photo: Statue of Martin Luther in front of Wartburg Theological Seminary in Dubuque, Iowa. Photo by Mike Haviland.

ISBN 0-8066-5111-3

The paper used in this publication meets the minimum requirements of American National Standard for Information Sciences—Permanence of Paper for Printed Library Materials, ANSI Z329.48-1984. ♾ ™

Manufactured in the U.S.A.

09   08   07   06   05   1   2   3   4   5   6   7   8   9   10

For Sarah

Contents

Acknowledgments

This book has received the support and encouragement of many individuals and institutions. First, I thank those closest to me, my family—Ann and our children Sarah, John, and Mary. You make me think Luther might have been right (even though I wish he would have been nicer about it): "People who do not like children are swine, dunces, and blockheads . . . they despise the blessing of God, the Creator and Author of marriage."

Second, I thank the numerous friends, colleagues, and mentors who have encouraged this work. Some now luxuriate with the church triumphant, while some still march with the church militant: Mary Gaebler, Heiko Oberman, Martha Stortz, Bradley Holt, Jonathan Strom, Loyd Allen, Hans-Juergen Hoepke, Hans Hillerbrand, Oswald Bayer, Dorothy Bass, Patrick Graham, Dennis Bielfeldt, Timothy Lull, and Martin Marty. I thank especially my "*Doktor-Vater*," George Forell, who has inspired my work and me for over three decades. I thank also, two special groups: "The Problem Keepers" and "The 'Bago Boys."

Third, I thank the congregations I have served. In many ways, this book grows out of the ministry we shared together in the University Lutheran Center at North Dakota State; Bethel Lutheran in Porter, Minnesota; Hemnes Lutheran in Minneota, Minnesota; and Lutheran Church of the Redeemer in Atlanta, Georgia.

Fourth, I thank the institutions of higher learning that have provided much needed and appreciated support: Candler School of

Theology (Pitts Theology Library); McAfee School of Theology (Swilley Library); Concordia College (Ylvisker Library); and Midland Lutheran College.

Fifth, I thank those groups that have granted me the privilege of addressing the theme of Luther's catechetical link between doctrine and prayer: The Charis Ecumenical Center, Green Lake Lutheran Ministries, Emory University, The Tenth International Congress for Luther Research, Sixteenth Century Studies Conference, *Die Fruehe Neuzeit Interdiziplinaer*, the American Academy of Religion, and the Goethe Institute-German Cultural Center of Atlanta.

Sixth, I thank the Louisville Institute for its General Grant program, which provided generous funding for this project.

Though edited to fit the format of this book, portions of this manuscript were originally published as articles: "Prayer: The Practical Focus of Luther's Theology," in *Let Christ Be Christ: Theology, Ethics, and World Religions in the Two Kingdoms*, edited by Daniel Hamerlink (Huntington Beach, California: Tentatio Press, 1999); and "Martin Luther, Catechesis, and Prayer," from *Word and World* (winter 2000).

Soli deo Gloria,
William R. Russell

Preface

As a contribution to "Lutheran Voices," this book seeks to listen to the original Lutheran voice. Therefore, its design highlights three major documents in which Martin Luther articulates his view of prayer and the Christian life. The intention is to let the reformer himself "speak" about his proposal to reform how the church of his day prayed.

These documents contain material spanning some twenty years of Luther's intense involvement in one of the most complex and definitive epochs in human history. Therefore, they proceed chronologically. From his early integration of prayer into parish education and then on to his own personal practice of prayer, these writings mark Luther's path toward his distinctive understanding of prayer and the Christian life. They mark his path to the Reformation.

Further, these documents also bear a catechetical family resemblance. They show the reformer's emphasis on prayer in the context of his repeated attention to the catechism—what we might today call parish or Christian education. This attention led him eventually to write the Large and Small Catechisms of 1529, and then continue work on this theme for the rest of his reformation career. All the while, he kept pointing to his conviction that fundamentally, catechesis is to teach believers how to practice Christian prayer.

Ways to Read This Book

Those interested in "spirituality" or the practice of Christian prayer can learn here how Martin Luther himself prayed. The down-to-earth and practical way that Luther prayed is a model for how modern believers might pray. Readers might want to read the last selection first, and then read the others as the Spirit moves them.

Those interested in history can trace Luther's development as a reformer—how his attempts to reform the church's prayer life led, contrary to his intentions, to the breakup of western Christianity. In addition, history-types will appreciate that Luther's style and his approach to prayer compel him to refer to people and customs and institutions of his day. Such readers might want to begin with the first piece and read their way through to the end.

In addition, "idea-people" will find in these documents the major themes of Luther's thought—with the added bonus of their application to the everyday Christian life. Lutheran notions of "law and gospel," "justification by faith alone," "theology of the cross," the Christian as simultaneously "saint and sinner," are fleshed out by the reformer in concrete and practical ways. Such folks might want to target Luther's descriptions of his doctrinal and theological priorities in these writings—noting especially the continuities and discontinuities of his ideas over time.

Those who teach in congregations, in families, and in church schools will find that Luther writes also for them. The documents collected here show Luther's appropriation of the Catechism as a source for teaching about prayer and the Christian life. Teachers might want to note how the reformer's catechetical strategy integrates action with learning—practicing prayer as an outgrowth of reflection on the basic teachings of Christianity.

Introduction:
Martin Luther, Prayer,
and the Christian Life

Many people know that Martin Luther's impact on history was huge—that for good reason he made all those "Top-Ten Lists" of important persons in the second millennium. Many people know that Luther was a courageous reformer of church and society—that he stood up to the church and the empire, the two most powerful institutions of medieval Europe. Many people know that Luther was a great communicator—that he preached with power, wrote with clarity, and taught with profundity.

Many people do not know, however, that Martin Luther's impact, courage, and clarity grew out of his enduring interest in the down-to-earth practice of Christian prayer. Luther thought that Christian prayer mattered, so the reformer prayed. He also taught others how to pray. Luther regularly spoke and wrote about prayer in ways designed to connect the everyday lives of everyday people with the Word of God.

In order to help make this concrete connection for congregations and their members, Luther sought to reform how parishes taught the basics of the Christian faith. In other words, Luther sought to reform the Catechism. The Catechism, for the reformer, was more than a pamphlet of doctrines. Luther understood the Catechism as a summary of the Scriptures, a "Lay Bible"—what believers needed to know in order to live the Christian life in a self-conscious, intentional manner. For Luther, such a life necessarily involved prayer and so the reformer emphasized prayer in the context of his catechetical reforms.

We would do well to view Luther's Catechism as he did—as a handbook of theology and prayer, designed to guide Christians and lead believers to understand their entire lives as prayer.

Reforming Prayer and Theology

Throughout his public ministry as teacher and preacher, Luther worked to reform catechesis. Along the way, he forged an unbreakable link between prayer and sound theology. For example, through no small effort of his own, the reformer published his explanation of a chief part of the traditional Catechism, the Lord's Prayer, in 1519—the *Exposition of the Lord's Prayer.* This book originated in a series of sermons on the Lord's Prayer that the reformer preached during Lent of 1517 in the City Church of Wittenberg. Luther's colleague, Johann Agricola, took notes on those sermons, reworked and published them in early 1518. Even though Agricola's book went through five editions in its first year, Luther was not satisfied. The reformer, therefore, asked another colleague who had heard those sermons, Nicholas von Amsdorf, to publish his version, which appeared in May 1519.

Still, Luther could not leave this topic alone. He was too intent on reforming this vitally important part of the catechism. He preached another series of sermons on the Lord's Prayer in December 1518 and then wrote two more interpretations of it in early 1519. The reformer incorporated this further material into his own reworking of those sermons from the spring of 1517, which he published in April 1519—actually pre-empting Amsdorf's book by about a month!

Significantly, in the midst of this tumultuous period, Luther took the time to publish this catechetical material on the Lord's Prayer. When he could have simply let Agricola's or von Amsdorf's editions stand, he took pains to bring out his own work on prayer. For Luther, prayer was simply too important to his reformation agenda.

Luther's sermonic and catechetical focus on prayer continued. In May 1522, he built upon his previous attention to catechetical themes and published the *Personal Prayer Book*, a programmatic work for the early Lutheran reformation. After some significant introductory material, Luther then interpreted in order, the Ten Commandments ("the Law"), the Apostles' Creed ("the Gospel"), and the Lord's Prayer ("the Christian life"). This ordering of things, familiar to those schooled in Luther's Catechism, was at the time quite innovative.

Moreover, this innovative ordering of things points to the distinctive character of the Lutheran reformation. For Luther, the Law not only contains the basics of the Christian ethical code, it reveals sin and the need for divine forgiveness. The Apostles' Creed points to the creative, redeeming, and sanctifying work of God, reminding unworthy sinners that the forgiveness they need comes through Jesus Christ. The Christian life of prayer then grows out of the new relationship God establishes with believers.

In other words, the grace of God sets the forgiven sinner free to live in the context of the relationship established by God in Jesus Christ. That is, one might say, the Christian is free to live a life of prayer. As the reformer would have it, Christians direct faith toward God (the first three commandments) and then direct love toward their neighbors (the final seven commandments). Among other things, therefore, the believer prays in faith for strength to obey the Ten Commandments—to live a life of "faith active in love" (to quote George Forell's enduring synopsis of Luther's ethics).

The importance of what the reformer is doing here is hard to overestimate. His *Personal Prayer Book*, in many ways, represents a radical shift in the history of catechesis, the history of theology, the history of the church—and even the history of the world for that matter! This document shows that, for Luther, obedience to the law does not constitute the Christian life. Nor is such obedience a prerequisite or precondition for prayer (as the catechetical tradition had too often taught in the generations prior to Luther). For the reformer, rather, Christian prayer and the Christian life grow out of the gospel of the forgiveness of sin given in Jesus Christ. Prayer is indicative of a new Divine-human relationship, a relationship characterized ultimately by Divine mercy, grace, and forgiveness.

This is very close to the heart of the Lutheran reformation. This is what Luther strived to communicate throughout his adult life. From this core, Luther worked to reform the church, even though it led to his excommunication from the church and his condemnation by the empire.

It made perfect sense for Luther to put this theological insight into a book on prayer. For him, prayer provided the context in which such insights take on practical meaning and expression. That is why there is such an obvious and inseparable connection between what he understood as sound doctrine and the practice of prayer.

As important as the *Personal Prayer Book* was to Luther's developing sense of catechesis, it was not a catechism *per se*. The appearance of what Timothy Wengert has called, "Wittenberg's first catechism," had to wait until 1525 and the *Booklet for Laity and Children*.

The booklet moves the Lutheran reform of catechesis forward in significant ways. First, it blends the *Personal Prayer Book* with the reformer's *Exposition of the Lord's Prayer*. By doing so, it clearly emphasizes Christian prayer in the context of Christian education for all people—while preserving Luther's distinctive law/gospel structure of the Christian life and prayer.

Second, this booklet extends Luther's catechetical reform to include brief discussions of the sacraments in the context of what the document labels, "the Lay Bible." This brings together for the first time the "five chief parts" of Luther's catechism.

Third, the booklet provides morning and evening "blessings," as well as readings and prayers for daily work and meal times. The emphasis of this work puts prayer at the center of the Christian life. Therefore, as the Lutheran reformation of catechesis proceeded, it inseparably connected doctrine with the practice of Christian prayer in the context of the Christian life.

This reformation continued—reaching a high point in 1529, with the publication of the catechisms. By the time these documents appeared, Luther had been striving to reform the church for a decade and a half. In the midst of that struggle, the reformer had been working out his distinctive catechetical strategy, with its connection between the study of theology and the practice of Christian prayer.

How Luther Prayed

Luther was indeed fundamentally interested in helping Christians understand their lives in relationship to God revealed in Jesus Christ. This relational context of the Christian life is, for the reformer, the context for Christian prayer. This is why he was convinced that this practice was so important for the vitality of the church. This is why he preached and wrote and taught so much about prayer.

This is also why Luther wrote about how he himself prayed the catechism, in *A Simple Way to Pray* (1535). In this definitive piece, Luther responds to a question about prayer posed by his long-time barber in Wittenberg, Peter Beskendorf. In doing so, Luther reaches the summit of his catechetical initiatives. He shows specifically how the reformation of the church he envisioned expressed itself in the intimate catechetical connection between theology and prayer.

Luther recommends that his friend, Peter the barber—and by extension, all Christians—do what he does: use the catechism creatively as a guide to pray.

The reformer probably knew that Peter was not extraordinarily "holy" or "pious." Indeed, it may not have seemed to Luther that Peter acted completely out of character when, about the time this writing was published, the barber was arrested and convicted for killing his son-in-law. The circumstances of the crime did not deter Luther. The reformer let the publication go forward because he recognized that Peter, warts and all, was an earnest seeker. Luther responded with care to an honest question about prayer posed by a person who was, to use Luther's parlance, every bit as much a sinner as he was a saint.

Prayer as a dominant theme of his catechetical work shows up in such a clear and compelling form here that this writing can be seen as one of the most important to flow from Luther's pen. There is no clearer summary of Martin Luther's catechetical piety.

Luther's Simple Way to Pray

Luther describes the practice of Christian prayer in a way that focuses believers' attention on everyday life in the world, lived in the context of the relationship established with them by God in Jesus Christ. This relational dimension makes Christian prayer for Luther both a conscious, intentional practice; as well as a constant reality in the life of the believer.

Before he discusses the specific characteristics of prayer, however, Luther greets his friend with kindness, even offering a prayer, with an eye toward subsequent readers: "Dear Master Peter: I offer you as best I can what I do personally when I pray. May our Lord God grant to you and to everyone else the ability to do it better. Amen." With these words, Luther sets the tone for what is to follow.

The famous professor does not presume upon his own status or "talk down" to Peter. Luther shows a sense of mutuality and respect for the questioner and, by extension, all Christians who would pray. He recognizes that his ordination or advanced degree or notoriety do not necessarily make him better at praying than other Christians. The reformer writes as a fellow believer, offering a method of prayer that he has found helpful and instructive—realizing that others may certainly be better at it than he is.

This tone continues as Luther admits that his own life of prayer is not always as robust or rewarding as he would like. He does not say piously, "I cannot get on without spending three hours daily in prayer"—such a statement is out of character for Luther (notwithstanding the fact that this oft-attributed-to-Luther phrase is apocryphal and occurs nowhere in his works!). Rather, he writes straightforwardly, without pretense or false piety, that he can be "cold and disinterested in prayer because of various tasks or thoughts." This is one of the afflictions that confronts every Christian, because, Luther writes, "the flesh and the devil always impede and obstruct prayer."

For Luther, prayer is a conversation with God that begins by "listening" to God's Word. When the cares and distractions of life weigh him down and prayer is burdensome, Luther seeks the Word. When he realizes that he has neglected this most fundamental of all relationships, Luther knows that he needs to hear the Word. Therefore, Luther's first instinct is to go to church. He looks for a place to worship. In worship, believers gather around Word and sacrament. They gather to pray.

If no gathering of the faithful is to be had, then he "listens" to the Word in another way. He reads the Psalms (the ancient prayer book of God's people), recites the Ten Commandments, the Creed, etc. Luther does this, he says, "quietly to myself, and word-for-word." As the reformer puts it, he here seeks to "warm" his heart so that he might pray consciously, "intent upon the matter" at hand.

Conscious Christian Prayer

This conscious character of prayer has, for Luther, many dimensions. Indeed, he can be quite specific with his advice—as if he has had considerable hands-on experience with Christian prayer and its accompanying successes and failures. The reformer offers some tips that indicate the practicality of his conception of prayer. First, he recommends that Christians begin and end their days with prayer. He describes this realistically. If they put off prayer, then the press of daily commitments will too often crowd out the ability consciously to connect with God through prayer. It is too easy for believers to become "cold and disinterested" in prayer—precisely the situation Luther wants Christians to avoid. Therefore, Luther recommends that Christians intentionally surround their lives with prayer.

By beginning and ending the day with prayer, Luther provides a faithful framework for living as a Christian. Prayer defines the Christian's conscious life. These times of prayer are like brackets, upholding and containing what believers do with their waking hours.

Second, the consciousness or intentionality of his view of prayer prompts Luther even to mention the posture or stance one might assume for prayer. The reformer advises Peter to "kneel or stand with your hands folded and your eyes toward heaven and speak or think. . . ." The point is to focus one's attention, to be conscious of what one is doing, saying, and thinking.

Third, the center of Luther's conscious life of prayer is the structured way he "prays" the catechism. Once he has found a suitable time to pray and has assumed a prayerful position, Luther uses the three main sections of the catechism—preeminently the Lord's Prayer—as the basis for prayer. Christian prayer, for Luther, involves meditation upon those kinds of texts—engaging them as "bidding prayers," which move the one who prays beyond pet themes and personal peccadilloes. Christian Prayer, for Luther, is not the thoughtless repetition of meaningless phrases.

To help believers pray consciously, Luther proposes a method of "warming" the heart for prayer. In particular, he uses the first two parts of the Catechism, the Ten Commandments, and the Apostles' Creed, as means to prepare for praying the main prayer-text for Christians, the Lord's Prayer.

When praying the Ten Commandments, for example, Luther speaks of weaving each commandment into what he calls, "a garland of four strands": instruction, thanksgiving, confession, prayer. The reformer then offers samples of how one might consciously pray the Commandments in this way. The method is consistent throughout. Luther first looks for what the Word has to teach him. Second, Luther thanks God for the lesson learned. Third, Luther confesses his own inability to obey. Fourth, Luther prays for the strength and the help to live according to the commandment under consideration.

Likewise, the reformer recommends praying through the Apostles' Creed. However, he knows that such a practice can overwhelm those unfamiliar with it. Luther's view of prayer here is nothing, if not realistic. He knows that, as important as conscious Christian prayer might be, it can become a burden if the believer tries to accomplish too much, be too pious. Therefore, he tells Peter that this method is "intended to help the heart come to itself and grow zealous in prayer. Take care, however, not to undertake all of this or so much that one becomes weary in spirit. . . . It is enough to consider one section or half a section which kindles a fire in the heart."

Once this takes place, once the Spirit has used the Word to kindle a fire in the heart of the believer, then Luther urges Peter to pray the Lord's Prayer consciously, giving each word and phrase due attention. He divides the Lord's Prayer into nine parts: the salutation ("Our Father in Heaven"), seven petitions, and the conclusion ("Amen"). Each part is worthy of the focused attention of the believer.

This way of praying is conscious. It makes use of the structure and content of the Catechism in order to assist believers as they pray. Luther is clear that what he offers Peter [and us] is a model, a proposal, a direction for praying or meditating on the Catechism. He does not want others to mimic him or thoughtlessly restate his words. Such "prayer" would betray the reformation of catechesis that he had spent his career trying to accomplish.

All of this describes the intentionality, the self-conscious structure, with which Luther prays. However, the reformer adds another dimension to his conscious method of prayer—creativity and freedom. Luther prays the catechism like a skilled musician who begins with a theme, improvises, builds on it, explores possibilities, and pushes edges, only to return to the base melody. This is what bidding prayers do: beckon pray-ers to examine areas of life and faith they might not otherwise.

This leads to a fifth dimension of Luther's self-conscious way to pray—listening to the Holy Spirit. For Luther, Christian prayer, based on the Word of God, involves sensitivity to the Holy Spirit. The Spirit, says Luther, may interrupt the Christian's prayers, in order to "preach" to the one who is praying. Luther describes this as getting " . . . lost among so many ideas in one petition that I pass on the other six . . . [because] one word of the Spirit's sermon is far better than a thousand of our prayers."

The Constancy of Christian Prayer

Prayer, for Luther, is a conscious, intentional act. At the same time, prayer is a constant reality. Christian prayer is living in and out of the relationship established with believers by God in Jesus Christ. Even neglecting the practice of prayer communicates something to God—that is, such neglect is a sort of prayer. Sometimes prayer involves conscious conversation. Sometimes prayer involves faithful and focused action in the world. From this standpoint, the entire Christian life is, for Luther, prayer. It involves conscious listening and responding to God's Word. Prayer also involves living out one's calling in the world.

The key here is the relational component of Luther's concept of prayer. Sometimes in relationships, the parties involved set dates and make appointments. Sometimes they scrap their agenda early on and address issues they had not planned on ahead of time. Sometimes they bump into one another and strike up a conversation. Sometimes in relationships, the various parties express themselves profoundly without words and through actions. These dynamics are at work in Luther's proposal for the reformation of prayer and the Christian life.

The sources collected here show how Luther cared deeply about prayer and the Christian life—about congregations, their people, and how they prayed. These writings grew out of his continuing efforts to reform the church through the congregation-based integration of sound doctrine with the practical practice of Christian prayer. This concern and these efforts, in many ways, define Martin Luther's work and explain his contribution to the church and the world.

Reflection Questions

1. Until reading this introduction, how do you understand Luther's importance in history?

2. Most interpretations of Martin Luther's life and work do not emphasize his attention to prayer and catechesis. Why do you think that may be true?

3. Who taught you how to pray?

4. How would you describe your current "prayer life"? What expectations do you bring to reading some of Luther's writings on the subject of prayer?

5. Consider keeping a journal of insights as you read the selected texts in the next three chapters.

1

Personal Prayer Book

1522

Luther published this "proto-catechism" in the midst of one of the most intense periods of the Reformation struggle—in the weeks immediately after he returned to Wittenberg from his hiding place at the Wartburg Castle. Its "law-gospel" scheme reorders the catechetical tradition of "Lord's Prayer, Creed, and Ten Commandments" (with emphasis on keeping the commandments) to "Ten Commandments, Creed, Lord's Prayer" (with Luther's possessive emphasis on believing the gospel of the forgiveness of sin). Luther here makes use of the popular late-medieval tradition of prayer books, in order to reform it.

This piece went through twenty-three editions between 1522 and 1530, and Luther continued to refer to it as an important summary of his teaching. The following is a revised version of the translation found in Luther's Works, volume 43, pages 5-45. Not included here are some materials that were later added to the ending by Luther or the printer.

❀

To all my dear masters and brothers in Christ, grace and peace:

Among the many harmful books and doctrines, which are misleading and deceiving Christians and give rise to countless false beliefs, I regard the personal prayer books as by no means the least objectionable. They drub into the minds of simple people such a wretched counting up of sins and going to confession, such un-Christian tomfoolery about prayers to God and his saints! Moreover, these books are puffed up with promises of indulgences and come out with decorations in red ink and pretty titles; one is called "a garden of the spirit", another "paradise of the soul", and so on. These books need a basic and thorough reformation if not total extermination. And I would make the same judgment about those passionals or books of legends into which the devil has tossed his own additions.

But I just don't have the time to undertake such a reformation; it is too much for me alone. So until God gives me more time and grace, I will limit myself to the exhortation in this book. To begin with, I offer this simple Christian form of prayer and mirror for recognizing sin, based on the Lord's Prayer and the Ten Commandments.

And I am convinced that when a Christian rightly prays the Lord's Prayer at any time or uses any portion of it as he may desire, his praying is more than adequate. What is important for a good prayer is not many words, as Christ says in Matthew 6 [:7], but rather a turning to God frequently and with heartfelt longing, and doing so without ceasing [I Thess. 5:17].

And herewith I urge everyone to break away from using the Bridget prayers and any others which are ornamented with indulgences or rewards and urge all to get accustomed to praying this plain, ordinary Christian prayer. The longer one devotes himself to this kind of praying, the more pleasant and dear it becomes. To that end may this prayer's Master, our dear Lord Jesus Christ, help us, to whom be blessings in all eternity. Amen.

∼

Foreword

It was not unintended in God's particular ordering of things that a lowly Christian person who might be unable to read the Bible should nevertheless be obligated to learn and know the Ten Commandments, the Creed, and the Lord's Prayer. Indeed, the total content of Scripture and preaching and everything a Christian needs to know is quite fully and adequately comprehended in these three items. They summarize everything with such brevity and clarity that no one can complain or make any excuse that the things necessary for his salvation are too complicated or difficult for him to remember.

Three things a person must know in order to be saved. First, he must know what to do and what to leave undone. Second, when he realizes that he cannot measure up to what he should do or leave undone, he needs to know where to go to find the strength he requires. Third, he must know how to seek and obtain that strength.

It is just like a sick person who first has to determine the nature of his sickness, then find out what to do or to leave undone. After that he has to know where to get the medicine which will help him do or leave undone what is right for a healthy person. Then he has to desire to search for this medicine and to obtain it or have it brought to him.

Thus the commandments teach man to recognize his sickness, enabling him to perceive what he must do or refrain from doing, consent to or refuse, and so he will recognize himself to be a sinful and wicked person. The Creed will teach and show him where to find the medicine—grace—which will help him to become devout and keep the commandments. The Creed points him to God and his mercy, given and made plain to him in Christ. Finally, the Lord's Prayer teaches all this, namely, through the fulfillment of God's commandments everything will be given him. In these three are the essentials of the entire Bible.

We begin with the commandments and there learn to perceive our sin and wickedness, that is, our spiritual sickness which prevents us from doing or leaving undone as we ought.

The First Tablet

Properly, the first or right-hand tablet of the commandments includes the first three, which instruct a person concerning his duty toward God—what he should do or leave undone, how he should conduct himself in relation to God.

The First Commandment teaches a person the right attitude in his own heart toward God, that is, what he should always keep in mind and consider important. Thus a person should expect all good things from God as from a father or good friend whom he trusts, loves, and respects at all times. And hence he should not offend God, just as a child avoids offending his father. Nature shows us that there is a God who grants every good thing and who helps in all trouble; even the heathen have their false gods, as the First Commandment says: "You shall have no other gods."

The Second Commandment teaches how a person should govern himself in relation to God both in his outward speech to others and also in his inward, personal attitude, that is, he should honor God's name. For no one can express God's divine nature, either to himself or to others, except by using God's name. Thus this commandment says: "You shall not take the name of your God in vain."

The Third Commandment teaches how a person should govern his actions toward God, that is, in worshiping. It says: "You shall sanctify the Day of Rest." In this way these three commandments teach a person how to govern himself toward God in thought and deed, in word and action, that is, in all of life.

The Second Tablet

The second or left hand tablet of the commandments includes the following seven commandments, in which a person is taught his obligation toward his fellow man and neighbor, what he should do and leave undone.

The first teaches how to govern oneself toward everyone in authority—those who act in God's place [Rom. 13:1–6; Eph. 6:5–8]. Hence this commandment comes immediately after the first three which relate to God himself, and it deals with those who are like God—father and mother, master and mistress. It says: "You shall honor your father and your mother."

The next commandment teaches how to deal with the person of our neighbor and fellow man, not harming him, but helping and assisting him whenever he needs it. It says: "You shall not kill."

The third teaches a person how to act in relation to what, next to his person, is his neighbor's most valuable possession—his wife, or child, or friend. We must not bring them into disgrace but preserve their reputation as much as we can. The commandment says: "You shall not commit adultery."

The fourth teaches a person how to act with regard to his neighbor's worldly property. One should not steal it or allow a loss, but help him prosper. It says: "You shall not steal."

The fifth teaches a person how to act toward his neighbor's worldly reputation and honor, not to weaken but to support, protect, and preserve it. It says: "You shall not give false testimony against your neighbor."

What is thus forbidden is harming one's neighbor in anything he owns; rather one should help him prosper. When we look at natural law, we see how right and universal the commandments all are. They require nothing toward God or our neighbor but that which anyone would want to see done, either from a divine or from a human point of view.

The last two commandments teach how evil our nature is and how unstained we should keep ourselves from all desires of the flesh and from avarice—for us a lifelong task and struggle. These commandments read: "You shall not covet your neighbor's house. You shall not covet his wife, his servants or maids, his livestock, or anything that is his."

In Matthew 7 [:12] Christ himself summarizes the Ten Commandments briefly, saying, "Whatever you want others to do to you, do the same to them; this is the whole Law and the Prophets." No one wants to see his kindness repaid by ingratitude or have someone defame his name. No one wants to be treated arrogantly, no one wants to be disobeyed, or treated with anger, or to have an unchaste wife, or to be robbed of his possessions, or endure falsehood against himself, or be betrayed, or be slandered. On the contrary, everyone wants his neighbor to show love and friendship, gratitude and helpfulness, truthfulness and loyalty—all required by these commandments.

What It Means to Break the Commandments
Breaking the First

Whoever tries to do away with trouble by witchcraft, by the black arts, or by an alliance with the devil.

Whoever uses [magic] writings, signs, herbs, words, spells, and the like.

Whoever uses divining rods, travels by a magic cloak, or steals milk, uses incantations to find treasure, resorts to crystal-gazing.

Whoever governs his life and work according to certain days, celestial signs, and the advice of fortune-tellers [Lev. 20:6].

Whoever uses certain incantations as blessings and charms against danger from wolves, sword, fire, or water to protect himself, his cattle, his children, and any kind of property.

Whoever ascribes any bad luck or unpleasantness to the devil or to evil persons and does not, in a spirit of love and praise, accept both evil and good as coming from God alone [Phil. 4:11], responding to God with gratitude and willing submission.

Whoever tempts God and exposes himself to unnecessary danger to body [Luke 4:12] and soul.

Whoever shows arrogance because of his piety, knowledge, or other spiritual gifts.

Whoever honors God and the saints only to gain some temporal advantage, forgetting the needs of his soul.

Whoever does not trust and rely upon God's mercy at all times and in everything he does.

Whoever doubts the Creed or God's mercy.

Whoever does not defend others against unbelief and doubt or does not do all in his power to help them believe and trust in God's mercy.

Here belongs every kind of doubt, despair, and false belief.

Breaking the Second Commandment

Whoever swears needlessly or habitually.

Whoever swears to support a falsehood or breaks his vow.

Whoever vows or swears to do evil.

Whoever uses God's name to curse.

Whoever tells silly stories about God and whoever carelessly misconstrues the words of Scripture.

Whoever does not call upon God's name in adversity and does not praise him in joy and sorrow, in fortune and misfortune [II Cor. 6:8].

Whoever uses his piety and wisdom to seek praise, honor, or reputation.

Whoever calls upon God's name falsely, as do heretics and all arrogant saints.

Whoever does not praise God's name, no matter what may happen to him.

Whoever does not restrain others from dishonoring God's name, from using it wrongly or for evil purposes.

Hence self-conceit, boasting, and spiritual pride belong here.

Breaking the Third Commandment

Whoever does not listen to God's word or try to understand it.

Whoever does not offer prayer to God.

Whoever does not regard all he does as God's work.

Whoever, in all he does and endures, does not quietly allow God to do with him as he pleases.

Whoever does not help the other person do all this and does not restrain him from doing otherwise.

Breaking the Fourth Commandment

Whoever is ashamed that his parents are poor, have faults, or are not highly regarded.

Whoever does not provide clothing and food for his needy parents.

Especially whoever curses or strikes his parents, slanders them, and is hateful and disobedient toward them.

Whoever does not in all sincerity regard them highly simply because God has so commanded.

Whoever does not hold his parents in honor even though they might do him wrong and even use force against him.

Whoever does not honor those in authority over him, remain loyal and obedient to them, no matter whether they are good or bad.

Whoever does not help others to obey this commandment and resist those who break it.

Here belongs every kind of arrogance and disobedience.

Breaking the Fifth Commandment

Whoever is angry with his neighbor.

Whoever says to him, "Raca" [Matt. 5:22]—which represents any expression of anger and hatred.

Whoever says to him, you nitwit, you fool [Matt. 5:22], that is, uses all sorts of insults, profanity, slander, backbiting, condemnation, scorn against his neighbor.

Whoever makes his neighbor's sin or shortcomings public rather than protecting him from publicity and trying to see the good in him.

Whoever does not forgive his enemies, does not pray for them, and whoever is unfriendly and does them no kindness.

Breaking this commandment includes all sins of anger and hatred, such as murder, war, robbery, arson, quarreling and feuding, begrudging a neighbor's good fortune and rejoicing over his misfortune [I Cor. 13:6].

Whoever fails to practice merciful deeds even toward his enemies [Matt. 5:44; Rom. 12:20].

Whoever sets persons against one another and incites them to strife [Prov. 16:28].

Whoever causes disunity between persons.

Whoever does not reconcile those who are at odds with one another [Matt. 5:9].

Whoever does not prevent or forestall anger and discord wherever he can.

Breaking the Sixth Commandment

Whoever violates virgins, commits adultery, incest, and similar kinds of sexual sins.

Whoever commits sexual perversions (called the unnamed sins) [Rom. 1:26-27; Lev. 18:22-23; 20:10-16].

Whoever uses lewd words, ditties, stories, pictures to incite others to sexual lust or displays such lust himself.

Whoever stirs up sexual desires in himself and contaminates himself by ogling, touching, and sexual fantasies.

Whoever does not avoid provocation to sexual sins—heavy drinking and eating, laziness and idleness, sleeping too much, and associating with persons of the opposite sex.

Whoever incites others to unchastity by excessive personal adornment, suggestive gestures, and other means.

Whoever allows his house, room, time, or assistance to be used for such sexual sins.

Whoever does not do and say what he can to help another person to be chaste.

Breaking the Seventh Commandment

Whoever steals, robs, and practices usury.

Whoever uses short weights and measures [Deut. 25:15], or who passes off poor merchandise as good.

Whoever gets an inheritance or income by fraud.

Whoever withholds earned wages [Deut. 24:15] and whoever refuses to acknowledge his debts.

Whoever refuses to lend money without interest to a needy neighbor.

All who are avaricious and want to get rich quickly.

Whoever in any way keeps what belongs to another or keeps for himself what is only entrusted to him for a time.

Whoever does not try to prevent loss to another person.

Whoever does not forewarn his neighbor against possible loss.

Whoever hinders what is advantageous to his neighbor.

Whoever is vexed by his neighbor's increase in wealth.

Breaking the Eighth Commandment

Whoever conceals and suppresses the truth in court.

Whoever does harm by untruth and deceit.

Whoever uses flattery to do harm, or spreads gossip, or uses double-talk.

Whoever brings his neighbor's conduct, speech, or wealth into question or disrepute.

Whoever allows others to speak evil about his neighbor, helps them, and does nothing to oppose them.

Whoever does not speak up in defense of his neighbor's good repute.

Whoever does not take a backbiter to task.

Whoever does not speak well about all his neighbors and does not keep silent about what is bad about them.

Whoever conceals the truth or does not defend it.

Breaking the Last Two Commandments

The last two commandments set a goal or target which we should attain. Daily and penitently we must strive toward this goal with God's help and grace because our evil desires will not die completely until our flesh is reduced to dust and then created anew.

The five senses are comprehended in the Fifth and Sixth Commandments; the six works of mercy in the Fifth and Seventh; the seven mortal sins—pride in the First and Second, lust in the Sixth, wrath and hatred in the Fifth, gluttony in the Sixth, sloth in the Third, and, for that matter, in all of them. The strange sins are covered by all the commandments, for it is possible to break all the commandments just by talking, advising, or helping someone. The crying and silent sins are committed against the Fifth, Sixth, and Seventh Commandments. In all of these deeds we can see the same thing: love of self which seeks its own advantage, robs both God and one's neighbor of their due, and concedes neither to God nor man anything they have, or are, or could do or become. Augustine expressed this succinctly when he said, "Self-love is the beginning of every sin."

The conclusion of all this is that the commandments demand or forbid nothing other than "love." Only "love" fulfills and only "love" breaks the commandments. Therefore St. Paul declares that "love is the fulfilling of the law" [Rom. 13:8-10], just as an "evil love" breaks all the commandments.

Fulfilling the Commandments
The First

Fear and love God in true faith, at all times, firmly trusting him in all that he does, accepting in simple, quiet confidence everything whether good or bad. What all of Scripture records about faith and hope and the love of God [I Cor. 13:13] belongs here and is briefly comprehended in this commandment.

The Second

Praise, honor, glorify, and call upon God's name, and rather sink into utter nothingness so that God alone be exalted, who is in all things and works in everything [Rom. 8:28, 11:36; Eph. 4:6]. Here belongs all that Scripture teaches about giving glory, honor, and thanksgiving to God and rejoicing in him.

The Third

Yield to God so that all we do is done by him alone through us. This commandment requires a person to be poor in spirit [Matt. 5:3], to sacrifice his nothingness to God so that He may be that sours only God and that in that soul God's deeds may be glorified [II Cor. 9:13] as the first two commandments require. Here belongs everything required of us: serving God, listening to what is preached about God, doing good deeds, subjecting the body to the spirit [I Cor. 9:27]. And so that all we accomplish is God's and nothing our own.

The Fourth

Show a willing obedience, humility, submissiveness to all authority as pleasing to God, as the Apostle St. Peter says [I Pet. 2:13], without protesting, complaining, and murmuring. Here belongs all that Scripture says regarding our obedience, humility, submissiveness, and giving honor.

The Fifth

Patience, meekness, kindness, peaceableness, mercy, and in every circumstance a tender and friendly heart, devoid of all hatred, anger, bitterness toward any person, even our enemies. Here belong all precepts concerning patience, meekness, peace, and harmonious relationships with others.

The Sixth

Chastity, decency, modesty in deeds, speech, attitude, and thought. Also moderation in eating, drinking, sleeping, and doing whatever encourages chastity. Here belong all precepts concerning sexual restraint, fasting, sobriety, temperance, praying, being vigilant, working hard, and whatever else furthers sexual restraint.

The Seventh

To be poor in spirit [Matt. 5:3], generous, willing to lend or give of our possessions, and to live free of avarice and covetousness. Here belongs all that is to be taught about avarice, fraudulent gain, deceit, craftiness, or allowing harm to happen to or hindering our neighbor's keeping what belongs to him.

The Eighth

A peaceful and beneficial manner of speech which harms no one and benefits everyone, reconciles the discordant, excuses and defends the maligned, that is, a manner of speech which is truthful and sincere. Here belong all precepts concerning when to keep silent and when to speak in matters affecting our neighbor's reputation, rights, concerns, and happiness.

The Last Two

They mean: perfect chastity and thorough disregard for all temporal pleasures and possessions—something not attainable until we reach the life beyond this one.

In all such actions we see nothing but a strange, all-comprehending love toward God and our neighbor which never seeks its own advantage but only what serves God and our neighbor [I Cor. 13:5]. It means to devote oneself freely to belonging to one's neighbor and serving him and his concerns.

Now you see that the Ten Commandments contain in a brief and orderly manner all precepts needful for a person's life. Anyone wishing to keep them all will find enough good deeds to do to fill every hour of the day; he need not hunt for other things to do, running here and there to do things which are not commanded [in Scripture].

We have clearly emphasized that these commandments prescribe nothing that man is to do or leave undone for his own advantage, or expect of others for himself, but rather what a person is to do or leave undone toward his neighbor, toward God, and toward his fellow man. Therefore we must comprehend the fulfillment of the commandments as meaning love for others and not for ourselves. For a person is more than enough inclined to occupy himself with whatever benefits himself as things are. He needs no precepts for doing this, but needs to be restrained in this direction. The person who lives the best life does not live for himself; he who lives for himself lives the most dastardly kind of life. This is what the Ten Commandments teach and they show us how few persons really live a good life, yes, that not one person is able to live this good life. Now that we recognize this, we must find out where to get the [medicinal] herbs to enable us to live a good life and fulfill the commandments.

Jesus
The Creed

The Creed is divided into three main parts, each telling about one of the three persons of the holy and divine Trinity. The first—the Father; the second—the Son; and the third—the Holy Spirit. The latter is the most important article of the Creed; all the others are based on it.

Notice here that faith is exercised in two ways. First, a faith about God meaning that I believe that what is said about God is true, just as I might say I believe that what people say about the Turks, the devil, and hell is true. This kind of believing is more an item of knowledge or an observation than a creed. The second kind of faith means believing in God—not just that I believe that what is said about God is true, but that I put my trust in him, that I make the venture and take the risk to deal with him, believing beyond doubt that what he will be toward me or do with me will be just as they [the Scriptures] say. I do not believe in this manner regarding any person, no matter how highly he be praised. It is easy for me to believe that a certain man is outstandingly religious, but that is no reason for me to build [my life] upon him. Only a faith that ventures everything in life and in death on what is said [in Scripture] of God makes a person a Christian and obtains all he desires from God. No corrupt or hypocritical heart can have such a faith; this is a living faith as the First Commandment demands: I am your God; you shall have no other gods.

So that little word *in* is well chosen and should be noted carefully; we do not say, I believe God the Father, or I believe about the Father, but rather, I believe *in* God the Father, *in* Jesus Christ, *in* the Holy Spirit. And this faith is given only by God himself and through it we confess the deity of Christ and of the Holy Spirit, thus believing in the Holy Spirit just as we do in the Father. And just as there is one faith in three Persons so the three Persons are one God.

The First Part of the Creed
I believe in God, the Father almighty, maker of heaven and the earth.
This means: I renounce the evil spirit, all idolatry, all sorcery, and all false belief.

I put my trust in no person on earth, not in myself, my power, my skill, my possessions, my piety, nor in anything else I may have.

I place my trust in no creature, whether in heaven or on earth.

I take the risk of placing my confidence only in the one, invisible, inscrutable, and only God, who created heaven and earth and who alone is superior to all creation. Again, I am not terrified by all the wickedness of the devil and his cohorts because God is superior to them all.

I would believe in God not a bit less if everyone were to forsake me and persecute me.

I would believe in God no less if I were poor, unintelligent, uneducated, despised, or lacking in everything.

I believe no less though I am a sinner. For this manner of faith will of necessity rise over all that does or does not exist, over sin and virtue and all else, thus depending purely and completely upon God as the First Commandment enjoins me to do.

I do not ask for any sign from God to put him to the test.

I trust in him steadfastly, no matter how long he may delay, prescribing neither a goal, nor a time, nor a measure, nor a way [for God to respond to me], but leaving all to his divine will in a free, honest, and genuine faith.

If he is almighty, what could I lack that God could not give or do for me?

If he is the Creator of heaven and earth and Lord over every thing, who, then, could deprive me of anything, or work me harm [Rom. 8:31]? Yes, how can it be otherwise than that all things work for good for me [Rom. 8:28] if the God, whom all creation obeys and depends upon, is well intentioned toward me?

If he is God, he can and wishes to do what is best with me. Since he is Father, he will do all this and do it gladly.

And since I do not doubt this but place my trust in him, I am assuredly his child, servant, and eternal heir, and it will be with me as I believe.

The Second Part

And in Jesus Christ, his only Son, our Lord: who was conceived by the Holy Spirit, born of the virgin Mary, suffered under Pontius Pilate, was crucified, dead, and buried: he descended into hell, the third day he rose from the dead, he ascended into heaven, and is seated on the right hand of God, the Father almighty, whence he shall come to judge the living and the dead.

I do not only believe that this means that Jesus Christ is the one true Son of God, begotten of him in eternity with one eternal divine nature and essence—but I also believe that the Father has made all things subject to him, that according to his human nature he has been made one Lord over me and all things which he created together with the Father in his divinity.

I believe that no one can believe in the Father and that no one can come to him by any ability, deeds, understanding, or anything that may be named in heaven or on earth [Eph. 3:15]. Rather, this faith is possible only in and through Jesus Christ, his only Son, that is, through faith in his name and lordship.

I firmly believe that for my welfare Christ was conceived by the Holy Spirit, by no human or carnal act and without any physical father or seed of man, so that he gives me and all who believe in him a pure, spiritual being, cleansing me of my sinful, carnal, impure, damnable conception [Ps. 51:5]—all this through his and the Almighty Father's gracious will.

I believe that for my sake he was born of the immaculate Virgin Mary, without changing her physical and spiritual virginity, so that according to his fatherly mercy he might render my sinful and damnable birth blessed, innocent, and pure, as he does for all his believers.

I believe that for my sin and the sin of all believers Christ bore his suffering on the cross and thereby transformed all suffering and every cross into a blessing—doing [the believer] no harm and even being salutary and most beneficial [for him].

I believe that Christ died and was buried to put my sin to death [II Tim. 1:10] and bury it and do the same for all believers and, moreover, that he slew human death [I Cor. 15:26], transforming it into something that does no harm and is beneficial [Phil. 1:10] and salutary [for the believer].

I believe that for me and all his believers Christ descended into hell to subdue the devil [I Pet. 3:18-20] and take him captive along with all his power, cunning, and malice so that the devil can no longer harm me, and that he redeemed me from the [eternal] pains of hell, transforming them into something nondestructive and beneficial [for the believer].

I believe that he was resurrected from the dead on the third day to give a new life to me and all believers, thus awakening us with him by his grace and spirit henceforth to sin no more [Rom. 6:4; Gal. 2:20] but to serve him only with every grace and virtue, thus fulfilling God's commandments.

I believe that he ascended into heaven and received power and honor over all angels and creatures [Phil. 2:9-10] and now sits at God's right hand [Eph. 1:20-22]. This means that he is King and Lord over all that is God's in heaven, earth, and hell. Hence he can help me and all believers against all troubles and against every adversary and foe [Rom. 8:38-39].

I believe that Christ will return from heaven on the Last Day to judge those who are alive at that time and those who have died before that day [I Thess. 4:16-17], that all mankind, angels, and devils will have to appear before his judgment throne [Matt. 18:35; Rom. 14:10; I Pet. 1:17] to see him visually. Then he will redeem me and all who believe in him from bodily death and every infirmity and will eternally punish his enemies and adversaries and deliver us from their power forever [Rev. 20:11-14].

The Third Part

I believe in the Holy Spirit, one holy Christian church, one communion of saints, one forgiveness of sins, resurrection of the body, and life everlasting. Amen.

I believe not only what this means—that the Holy Spirit is truly God together with the Father and the Son—but also that except through the Holy Spirit's work no one can come in and to the Father through Christ and his life, his suffering and death, and all that is said [in Scripture] of him, nor can anyone appropriate any of this to himself. Working through the Spirit, Father and Son stir, awaken, call, and beget new life in me and in all who are his. Thus the Spirit in and through Christ quickens, sanctifies, and awakens the spirit in us and brings us to the Father, by whom the Spirit is active and life-giving everywhere.

I believe that throughout the whole wide world there is only one holy, universal, Christian church, which is nothing other than the gathering or congregation of saints—pious believers on earth. This church is gathered, preserved, and governed by the same Holy Spirit and is given daily increase by means of the sacraments and the word of God.

I believe that no one can be saved who is not in this gathering or community, harmoniously sharing the same faith with it, the same word, sacraments, hope, and love. And that no Jew, heretic, pagan, or sinner can be saved along with this community unless he becomes reconciled with it and unites with it in full agreement in all things.

I believe that in this community or Christendom all things are held in common; what each one possesses belongs also to others and no one has complete ownership of anything. Hence, all the prayers and good deeds of all the Christian community benefit, aid, and strengthen me and every other believer at all times, both in life and in death, and that each one bears the other's burden, as St. Paul teaches [Gal. 6:2].

I believe that there is forgiveness of sin nowhere else than in this community and that beyond it nothing can help to gain it—no good deeds, no matter how many or how great they might be; and that within this community nothing can invalidate this forgiveness of sin—no matter how gravely and often one may sin; and that such forgiveness continues as long as this one community exists. To this [community] Christ gave the power of the keys, saying in Matthew 18 [:18], "Whatever you bind on earth shall be bound in heaven." He said the same to Peter as an individual, representing and taking the place of one and only one church, "[I will give you the keys of the kingdom of heaven, and] whatever you bind on earth," etc., Matthew 16 [: 18–19].

I believe that there will be a resurrection from the dead in the future in which all flesh will be raised from the dead through the Holy Spirit, that is, all mankind, good and evil, will be raised bodily to return alive in the same flesh in which they died, were buried, and decayed or perished in various ways.

I believe in an eternal life for the saints after the resurrection and in an eternal dying for the sinners. And I haven't a doubt about all this, that the Father through his Son Jesus Christ our Lord and with the Holy Spirit will let all this happen to me. I say Amen, that is, this is a sure and trustworthy truth.

The Lord's Prayer
Preface and Preparation for Praying the Seven Divine Petitions
   Our Father who art in heaven
   What this means:
   O Almighty God, in your unmerited goodness to us and through the merit and mediation of your only beloved Son, Jesus Christ, you have permitted and even commanded and taught us to regard you and call upon you as one Father of us all. You have done so although instead you could rightly and properly be a severe judge over us sinners since we have acted so often against your divine and good will and have aroused your wrath. Now through your mercy implant in our hearts a comforting trust in your fatherly love, and let us experience the sweet and pleasant savor of a childlike certainty that we may joyfully call you Father, knowing and loving you and calling on you in every trouble. Watch over us that we may remain your children and never become guilty of making you, dearest Father, our fearful judge, changing ourselves, your children, into your foes.

   You do not wish us just to call you Father but that we all, together, should call on you, Our Father. Therefore grant us a harmonious and brotherly love so that we may all regard and accept each other as true brothers and sisters and turn to you as the dear Father of us all, praying for all persons as one child might entreat his father for someone else. And let none of us seek only his own advantage in prayer before you, forgetting the other person, but let us strip ourselves of all hatred, envy, and discord, and love each other as true and reverent children of God, and thus all repeat together not *my* Father, but *our* Father.

Moreover, since you are not a physical father here on earth but a spiritual Father in heaven, not like an earthly, mortal father who is not always dependable and cannot be of help by himself, show us what an immeasurably better Father you are and teach us to regard earthly fatherhood, fatherland, friends, possessions, body and blood as far less in value than you. Grant us, O Father, that we may be your heavenly children, teach us to value only our spiritual and heavenly inheritance, lest we be deluded by an earthly father, fatherland, or by possessions into becoming merely children of this world. And grant that we might say with true conviction: O our heavenly Father, we are truly your heavenly children.

The First Petition
Hallowed be thy name

What this means:

O Almighty God, dear heavenly Father, in this wretched vale of tears your holy name is sadly profaned, blasphemed, and reviled in so many ways. In so many instances it is regarded without honor to you and is often misused in sinning, so that to live a disgraceful life might well be regarded as the same as disgracing and dishonoring your holy name.

Therefore grant us your divine grace that we might guard against all that does not serve to the honor and glory of your holy name. Help us to do away with all sorcery and magic incantations. Help us put an end to conjuring by the devil or other creatures by your name. Help us root out all false belief and superstition. Help us bring to naught all heresies and false doctrines which are spread under the guise of your name. Help that no one be deceived by the many kinds of falsehood which go under the pretense of truth, piety, and holiness. Help that no one may resort to using your name to swear, lie, or deceive. Protect us from all false and imaginary consolation which might be given in your name. Protect us against all spiritual arrogance and false pride based on temporal fame or reputation. Help us to invoke your holy name in all our troubles and infirmities. Help us not to forget your name when we lie on our deathbed and our conscience is troubled. Help that we may use all our possessions, speech, and deeds to glorify and honor you alone and that we do not seek to claim or seek a reputation in doing this, but that all we do be done for you to whom alone everything belongs. Protect us from the shameful vice of ingratitude.

Help that our good deeds and conduct may incite others to praise and honor you but not ourselves, exalting and praising your name because of us. Help us so that our evil actions and shortcomings may not offend anyone, leading them to dishonor your name or to neglect your praise. Protect us from asking you for anything temporal or eternal which would not serve the glory and honor of your name. Should we petition you in such a way, do not listen to our folly. Help us conduct all our life in such a way that we may be found to be true children of God, lest we call you Father falsely or in vain. Amen.

And in this prayer belong all psalms and prayers of praise, honor, and thanksgiving, all songs to his honor, and every alleluia.

The Second Petition
May thy kingdom come near

What this means:

This wretched life is a realm of every sin and malice, whose one lord is the evil spirit, the initiator and villainous instigator of all sin and wickedness. Yours is a realm, however, of every virtue and grace, whose one Lord is Jesus Christ, your dear Son, the Author and Beginner of every grace and truth. For this, dear Father, give us help and grace and above all else grant us a true and constant faith in Christ, a fearless hope in your mercy for overcoming all the stupidity of our sinful conscience. And grant a kindly love toward us and all mankind.

Protect us from unbelief, despair, and from boundless envy. Deliver us from the filthy lust of unchastity and grant us a love of every kind of virginity and chastity. Deliver us from discord, war, and dissension, and let the virtue, peace, harmony, and tranquillity of your kingdom draw near. Grant that anger or other bitterness does not reign over us, but that by your grace, genuine kindness, loyalty, and every kind of friendliness, generosity, and gentleness may reign in us. Grant that inordinate sadness and depression may not prevail in us, but let joy and delight in your grace and mercy come over us.

And finally may envy be averted from us and, being filled with your grace and with all virtues and good deeds, may we become your kingdom so that in heart, feeling, and thought we may serve you with all our strength inwardly and outwardly, obediently serving your purpose, being governed by you alone and never following self-love, the flesh, the world, or the devil.

Grant that your kingdom, begun in us, may daily increase and improve, lest cunning malice and apathy for doing good overcome us so that we slip back. Rather grant us both earnestly to resolve and to be able to make a beginning to live a pious life as well as to make vigorous progress in it and reach its goal. As the prophet says, "Lighten my eyes, lest I sleep the sleep of death or become slothful in the good life I have begun, lest my enemy say, 'I have prevailed over him.'"

Grant that we may thus remain steadfast and that your future kingdom may be the end and consummation of the kingdom you have begun in us. Help us get free from this sinful and perilous life. Help us to yearn for that future life and be a foe of this present life.

Help us not to fear death but to desire it. Turn us from love and attachment to this life so that in everything your kingdom may be accomplished in us.

To this petition belong all psalms, verses, and prayers which implore God for grace and virtue.

The Third Petition
Thy will be done equally in heaven and earth
What this means:

Compared with your will, ours is never good but always evil. Your will is at all times the best, to be cherished and desired above everything else. Therefore have mercy upon us, O dear Father, and let nothing happen just because it is our own will. Grant and teach us a deeply based patience in times when our will is prevented from happening or comes to nothing or when someone contradicts our will by what he says or does not say, does or leaves undone. Help us not to become angry or vexed, not to curse, complain, protest, condemn, disparage, or contradict [when what we will is not done]. Help us to yield humbly to our adversaries and those who obstruct our will, surrendering our own will. Help us to speak well of such adversaries, to bless them, and to do good to them as persons who are carrying out your best and godly purposes in contradiction to our own.

Grant us grace to bear willingly all sorts of sickness, poverty, disgrace, suffering, and adversity and to recognize that in this your divine will is crucifying our will. Help us also to endure injustice gladly and preserve us from taking revenge. Let us not repay evil with evil [Matt. 5:39; Rom. 12:19, 21] nor meet violence with violence, but rather let us rejoice that these things happen to us according to your will and so let us praise and give thanks to you [Matt. 5:11]. Let us not ascribe to the devil or to evil persons anything that happens contrary to our will, but solely ascribe this to your divine will which orders everything that may hinder our will in order to increase the blessedness of your kingdom. Help us to die willingly and gladly and readily accept death as your will so that we do not become disobedient to you through impatience or discouragement on our part.

Grant that we do not give our bodily members—eyes, tongue, heart, hands, and feet—free rein for what they desire or purpose, but make them captive to your will, bring them to a stop, and subdue them. Protect us from any kind of evil will—forward, stubborn, stiff-necked, or obstinate. Grant us true obedience, a perfect, calm, single-minded composure in all things—spiritual, earthly, temporal, and eternal. Protect us from the horrible vice of character assassination, slander, backbiting, frivolously judging or condemning others, and misrepresenting what others have said. O hold far from us the plague and tragedy which such speech can cause; rather, whenever we see or hear anything in others that seems wrong or displeasing to us, teach us to keep quiet, not to publicize it, and to pour out our complaints to you alone and to commit all to your will. And let us sincerely forgive all who wrong us and be sympathetic toward them.

Teach us to recognize that no one can harm us without first harming himself a thousand times more in your eyes, so that we might thus be moved more to pity rather than to anger toward such a person, to commiserate with him rather than count up his wrongs. Whenever those who did not do our will or did us harm in their conduct or otherwise displeased us are struck with adversity, help us to refrain from rejoicing. Also help us not to be saddened by their good fortune.

To this petition belongs every psalm, verse, or prayer which petitions for help against sin and our foes.

The Fourth Petition
Give us this day our daily bread

What this means:

This bread is our Lord Jesus Christ who feeds and comforts the soul [John 6:51]. Therefore, O heavenly Father, grant grace that the life, words, deeds, and suffering of Christ be preached, made known, and preserved for us and all the world. Help that we may find in his words and deeds an effective example and mirror of all virtues for every phase of life. Help that we may be strengthened and comforted in suffering and adversity in and through his suffering and cross. Help us through his death to overcome our own death with a firm faith and thus boldly follow our beloved Guide into the life beyond this one.

Graciously grant that all pastors preach your word and Christ throughout the world in a way effective for salvation. Help that all who hear the preaching of your word may learn to know Christ and thus sincerely lead better lives. May you also graciously drive out of the holy church all foreign doctrine and preaching which do not teach Christ.

Be merciful to all bishops, priests, other clergy, and to all in authority that illumined by your grace they may lead and teach us aright through speech and good example.

Protect all who are weak in faith that they may not be offended by the bad example set by those in authority.

Protect us against heretical and apostate teachers so that we may remain united in one daily bread—the daily teaching and word of Christ. By your grace teach us inwardly to contemplate Christ's suffering in a proper manner and rejoice to copy it in our lives. At our life's end do not let us be deprived of the holy and true body of Christ. Help all priests to administer and use the sacred sacrament worthily and blessedly for the betterment of all Christendom. Graciously help us and all other Christians to receive the holy sacrament at the proper time.

And in brief, give us our daily bread so that Christ may remain in us eternally and we in him [John 15:5], and that we may worthily bear the name of Christian as derived from Christ.

In this petition belong all prayers or psalms offered for those in authority and especially those directed against false teachers. Here belong also those petitions for the Jews, heretics, and all persons who err, also for the grief-stricken and those who suffer without hope.

The Fifth Petition

And do not hold us accountable for debts, as we do not hold our debtors accountable

What this means:

This petition has one condition: we must first forgive our debtors. When we have done that, then we may pray "forgive us our debts." That is what we prayed for earlier in the Third Petition—that God's will be done, to endure everything with patience, not to repay evil with evil, not to seek revenge, but to return evil with good as our Father in heaven does, who lets his sun rise on the good and the evil and sends rain to those who thank him and to those who do not [Matt. 5:45]. Therefore we implore you, O Father, to comfort us in the present and in the hour of our death when our conscience will be frightened terribly by our sins and by your judgment.

Grant your peace in our hearts that we may anticipate your judgment with joy. Let us not feel the harshness of your judgment for no one could then be found righteous before you [Ps. 143:2]. Teach us, dear Father, not to find reliance or consolation in good deeds or purposes, nor in merit, but teach us simply to venture all upon your boundless mercy, committing ourselves with utter firmness to it alone. Likewise, let not our guilty and sinful life bring us into despair, but may we regard your mercy as higher, broader, and stronger than anything in our life.

Help all who are in peril of death and despair, particularly those whom we name [in our prayer before you]. Have mercy upon all poor souls in purgatory, especially those we name [in our prayer]. Be forgiving of every guilt toward them and us all, comfort them, and take them under your mercy.

Repay our wickedness with your goodness, as you have commanded us to do [to others]. Silence that evil spirit—the cruel backbiter, accuser, end magnifier of our sin—now and in our last hour, and in every torment of conscience, just as we, on our part, hold back from slandering and magnifying the sins of others. Do not judge us according to the accusations the devil or our wretched conscience brings against us, and pay no heed to the voice of our enemies who accuse us day and night before you, just as in turn we will pay no heed to the slanders and accusations of others [against us].

Relieve us of every heavy burden of sin and conscience so that in life and death, in enduring and in doing we may trust in your mercy, completely and with a light and happy heart.

In this petition belong all psalms and prayers which invoke God's mercy for our sin.

The Sixth Petition
And lead us not into temptation

What this means:

Three temptations or trials confront us: the flesh, the world, and the devil. Hence we pray: Dear Father, grant us grace to overcome the fleshly lusts. Help that we may withstand excesses in eating, drinking, sleeping too much, idleness, and laziness. Help us to make constructive use of fasting, to be moderate in food, dress, and sleep, keeping alert in our doing and working. Help us, with Christ, to crucify and put to death the evil desire and inclination of the flesh [Rom. 6:6] so as not to yield to any temptations of the flesh or to follow them. Help that when we look at a beautiful person or picture or any other creature, that this may not bring us into temptation but rather be an occasion for cherishing chastity and praising you in your creatures. Help that when we hear or feel something pleasant and pleasurable that we do not seek to indulge our lust in this but rather to seek to praise and glorify you for it.

Protect us from the great vice of avarice and covetousness with regard to the riches of this world. Protect us from seeking honor and power in this world, or from even being inclined in this direction. Protect us that the deceit, delusion, and enticement of this world may not stir us to seek after them. Keep us that we be not drawn into impatience, vindictiveness, anger, or other vices by the world's evil and unpleasantness.

Help us renounce and forsake the world's deceit and delusion, allurements and fickleness—all its good or evil, as we vowed to do in baptism. Help that we may remain steadfast and grow in [the promise of our baptism] from day to day.

Protect us from the devil's whisperings so that we do not give in to pride, our own pleasure, and a contempt for others to gain wealth, high rank, power, skill, beauty, or any other blessing of yours. Preserve us from falling into hatred or envy for any reason whatsoever. Protect us against being governed by religious doubt and despair, now and at our last hour.

Heavenly Father, may all who work and struggle against these great and manifold temptations be committed to your care. Strengthen those who are unbowed, raise the fallen and the defeated. And in the wretched insecurities of this life, grant us all your grace that we, being surrounded by so many foes, may do battle with a firm and valiant faith, and may obtain an eternal crown.

The Seventh Petition
But deliver us from evil
What this means:

This petition bids for deliverance from every evil of pain and punishment, as the holy church does in the litanies. Deliver us, O Father, from your eternal wrath and from the pangs of hell. Deliver us, O Father, in death and on Judgment Day, from your severe condemnation. Deliver us from sudden death. Protect us from fire and flood, from lightning and hail. Protect us from hunger and famine. Protect us from war and bloodshed. Protect us when you send plagues, pestilence, venereal disease, and other grave sickness. Protect us from every bodily evil and woe, to the end, however, that all this may rebound to the honor of your name, the increase of your kingdom, and [the accomplishment] of your holy will. Amen.

Amen

God grant that we may obtain all these petitions with certainty. Let us not doubt that you have heard us in the past and will do so in the future, answering us with a Yes and not a No or a Maybe. Thus we cheerfully say Amen—this is true and certain. Amen.

The Hail Mary

Take note of this: no one should put his trust or confidence in the Mother of God or in her merits, for such trust is worthy of God alone and is the lofty service due only to him. Rather praise and thank God through Mary and the grace given her. Laud and love her simply as the one who, without merit, obtained such blessings from God, sheerly out of his mercy, as she herself testifies in the Magnificat [Luke 1:46–55].

It is very much the same when I am moved by a view of the heavens, the sun, and all creation to exalt him who created everything, bringing all this into my prayer and praise, saying: O God, Author of such a beautiful and perfect creation, grant to me. . . . Similarly, our prayer should include the Mother of God as we say: O God, what a noble person you have created in her! May she be blessed! And so on. And you who honored her so highly, grant also to me. . . .

Let not our hearts cleave to her, but through her penetrate to Christ and to God himself. Thus what the Hail Mary says is that all glory should be given to God, using these words: "Hail, Mary, full of grace. The Lord is with thee [Luke 1:28]; blessed art thou among women and blessed is the fruit of thy womb, Jesus Christ. Amen."

You see that these words are not concerned with prayer but purely with giving praise and honor. Similarly there is no petition in the first words of the Lord's Prayer but rather praise and glorification that God is our Father and that he is in heaven. Therefore we should make the Hail Mary neither a prayer nor an invocation because it is improper to interpret the words beyond what they mean in themselves and beyond the meaning given them by the Holy Spirit.

But there are two things we can do. First, we can use the Hail Mary as a meditation in which we recite what grace God has given her. Second, we should add a wish that everyone may know and respect her [as one blessed by God].

In the first place, she is full of grace, proclaimed to be entirely without sin—something exceedingly great. For God's grace fills her with everything good and makes her devoid of all evil.

In the second place, God is with her, meaning that all she did or left undone is divine and the action of God in her. Moreover, God guarded and protected her from all that might be hurtful to her.

In the third place, she is blessed above all other women, not only because she gave birth without labor, pain, and injury to herself, not as Eve and all other women, but because by the Holy Spirit and without sin, she became fertile, conceived, and gave birth in a way granted to no other woman.

In the fourth place, her giving birth is blessed in that it was spared the curse upon all children of Eve who are conceived in sin [Ps. 51:5] and born to deserve death and damnation. Only the fruit of her body is blessed, and through this birth we are all blessed.

Furthermore, a prayer or wish is to be added—our prayer for all who speak evil against this Fruit and the Mother. But who is it that speaks evil of this Fruit and the Mother? Any who persecute and speak evil against his work, the gospel, and the Christian faith, as Jews and papists are now doing.

The conclusion of this is that in the present no one speaks evil of this Mother and her Fruit as much as those who bless her with many rosaries and constantly mouth the Hail Mary. These, more than any others, speak evil against Christ's word and faith in the worst way.

Therefore, notice that this Mother and her Fruit are blessed in a twofold way—bodily and spiritually. Bodily with lips and the words of the Hail Mary; such persons blaspheme and speak evil of her most dangerously. And spiritually [one blesses her] in one's heart by praise and benediction for her child, Christ—for all his words, deeds, and sufferings. And no one does this except he who has the true Christian faith because without such faith no heart is good but is by nature stuffed full of evil speech and blasphemy against God and all his saints. For that reason he who has no faith is advised to refrain from saying the Hail Mary and all other prayers because to such a person the words apply: Let his prayer be sin [Ps. 109:7].

Psalm 12
To be prayed for the exaltation of the holy gospel
Psalm 67
To be prayed for the increase of faith
Psalm 51
Concerning the whole matter, that is, the essential and original sin together with its consequences
Psalm 103
For thanking God for all his goodness to us
Psalm 20
For good government and for earthly authorities
Psalm 79
Against the enemies of the Christian church and the gospel
Psalm 25
A general prayer to submit to God in all things
Psalm 10
To be prayed against the Antichrist and his kingdom

Reflection Questions

1. In his cover letter, Luther wrote that he did not have the time to seek the "thorough reformation" the practice of prayer needed in his day. Yet, that was the work to which God called him. Has God ever "surprised" you with a calling or an answer to your prayers you did not expect?

2. How does the medical metaphor Luther uses in the foreword to describe the "three things a person must know in order to be saved" work for you? In what ways is it useful and in what ways is it unhelpful?

3. Does it surprise you that Luther includes an interpretation of the "Hail Mary," in this work? Why?

4. How does Luther interpret "our daily bread," in the fourth petition of the Lord's Prayer?

5. What do you think of the idea of basing your daily prayers on a review of the key parts of the Catechism? In what ways may this be beneficial?

6. What, in particular, do you learn about prayer and how to pray from reading Luther's *Personal Prayer Book?*

2

Booklet for Laity and Children

1525

Luther's precise role in the compilation and publication of this work is not completely clear. It is clear, however, that this booklet grows out of the Lutheran reformation's focus on catechesis—teaching sound doctrine to all believers so they might pray aright. Furthermore, the booklet makes extensive and strategic use of both Luther's 1519 Exposition of the Lord's Prayer for Simple Lay Folks *and the* Personal Prayer Book.

Published at least twenty-six times, between 1525 and 1530, the booklet was to teach illiterate people the basics of the Christian faith—beginning with a woodcut of Jacob and the ladder of Angels, followed by a copy of the alphabet. The daily blessings and short meditation on the Lord's Prayer emphasize an evangelical understanding of the Christian life of prayer. The version here is condensed from Sources and Contexts of the Book of Concord, *ed. by Robert Kolb and James Nestingen (Fortress Press, 2001).*

The opening section called the "Lay Bible" compiles the key texts of the Small Catechism and thus are not repeated here. The concluding section, "On Confession," is also not included here.

∾

An Instruction

For all people to be saved three things are necessary. First, they must know what to do and what to leave undone. This is what the Ten Commandments teach.

Second, when they realize that they cannot measure up to what they should do or leave undone with their own powers, they need to know where to go to find the strength they require. This the Creed shows them.

Third, they must know how to seek and obtain that strength [namely through prayer. The Lord's Prayer teaches them this.].

On the Creed

The Creed is divided into three main parts, each telling about one of the three persons of the holy and divine Trinity. The first [is dedicated to] the Father, the second [to] the Son, and the third [to] the Holy Spirit. [For this] is the most important article of the Creed; all the others are based on it.

The First Part.
The Second Part.
The Third Part.

The First Part of the Creed

I believe in God, the Father almighty, maker of heaven and the earth. This means: I renounce the evil spirit, all idolatry, all sorcery, and all false belief.

I put my trust in no person on earth, not in myself, my power, my skill, my possessions, my [righteousness], nor in anything else I may have.

I place my trust in no creature, whether in heaven or on earth.

I set my hope and confidence only in the one, invisible, inscrutable, and only God, who created heaven and earth and who alone is superior to all creation. Again, I am not terrified by all the wickedness of the devil and his cohorts because my God is superior to them all.

I would believe in God not a bit less if everyone were to forsake me and persecute me.

I would believe in God no less if I were poor, unintelligent, uneducated, despised, or lacking in everything.

I believe no less though I am a sinner. For this manner of faith will of necessity rise over all that does or does not exist, over sin and virtue and all else, thus depending purely and completely upon God as the First Commandment enjoins me to do.

I do not ask for any sign from God to put him to the test.

I trust in him steadfastly, no matter how long he may delay, prescribing neither a goal nor a time, nor a measure, nor a way [for God to respond to me], but leaving all to his divine will in a free and genuine faith.

If he is almighty, what could I lack that God could not give or do for me?

If he is the Creator of heaven and earth and Lord over everything, who, then, could deprive me of anything, or cause me harm? Yes, how can it be otherwise than that all things work for good for me [Rom. 8:28] if the God, whom all creation obeys and depends upon, is well intentioned toward me?

Because he is God, he can and wishes to do what is best with me. Since he is Father, he will do all this and do it gladly.

And since I do not doubt this but place my trust in him, I am assuredly his child, servant, and eternal heir, and it will be with me as I believe.

The Second Part of the Creed

And in Jesus Christ, his only Son, our Lord: who was conceived by the Holy Spirit, born of the Virgin Mary, suffered under Pontius Pilate, was crucified, [died,] and was buried; he descended into hell, the third day he rose from the dead, he ascended into heaven, and is seated on the right hand of God, the Father almighty, whence he shall come to judge the living and the dead.

That is:

I do not only believe that this means that Jesus Christ is the one true Son of God, begotten of him in eternity with one eternal divine nature and essence—but I also believe that the Father has made all things subject to him, that according to his human nature he has been made one Lord over me and all things, which he created together with the Father in his divinity.

I believe that no one can believe in the Father and that no one can come to him by any ability, deeds, understanding, or anything that may be named in heaven or on earth, except alone in and through Jesus Christ, his only Son, that is, through faith in his name and lordship.

I firmly believe that for my welfare Christ was conceived by the Holy Spirit, apart from any human or carnal act and without any physical father or seed of man, so that he makes me and all who believe in him spiritual, cleansing me of my sinful, carnal, impure, damnable conception—all this through his and the almighty Father's gracious will.

I believe that for my sake he was born of the immaculate Virgin Mary, without changing her physical and spiritual virginity, so that according to his fatherly mercy he might render my sinful and damnable birth blessed, innocent, and pure, as he does for all his believers.

I believe that for my sin and the sin of all believers Christ bore his suffering on the cross and thereby brings blessing through every suffering and cross and has thus made them not only harmless but also salutary and highly rewarding.

I believe that Christ died and was buried to put my sin to death and bury it and do the same for all believers and, moreover, that he slew human death, transforming it into something that does no harm and is beneficial and salutary.

I believe that for me and all his believers Christ descended into hell to subdue the devil and take him captive along with all his power, cunning, and malice so that the devil can no longer harm me, and that he redeemed me from the pains of hell, transforming them into something harmless and beneficial.

I believe that he was resurrected from the dead on the third day to give a new life to me and all believers, thus awakening us with him by his grace and spirit henceforth to sin no more but to serve him only with every grace and virtue, thus fulfilling God's commandments.

I believe that he ascended into heaven and received power and honor over all angels and creatures and now sits at God's right hand. This means that he is King and Lord over all that is God's in heaven, earth, and hell. Hence he can help me and all believers against all troubles and against every adversary and foe.

I believe that Christ will return from heaven on the Last Day to judge those who are alive at that time and those who have died before that day, that all humankind, angels, and devils will have to appear before his judgment throne to see him with their eyes. Then he will redeem me and all who believe in him from bodily death and every infirmity and will eternally punish his enemies and adversaries and deliver us from their power forever.

The Third Part of the Creed

I believe in the Holy Spirit, one holy Christian church, one community of saints, forgiveness of sins, resurrection of the body, and eternal life. Amen.

That is:

I believe not only that the Holy Spirit is true God together with the Father and the Son, but also that except through the Holy Spirit's work no one can come in and to the Father through Christ and his life, his suffering and death, and all that is said of him [in the Creed], nor can anyone appropriate any of this to himself. Working through the Spirit, Father and Son stir up, awaken, call, and beget new life in me and in all who are his. Thus in and through Christ the Spirit quickens, sanctifies, and awakens the spirit in us and brings us to the Father, by whom the Spirit is active and life-giving everywhere.

I believe that throughout the whole wide world there is only one holy, universal, Christian church, which is nothing other than the gathering or congregation of saints—[righteous] believers on earth. This church is gathered, preserved, and governed by the same Holy Spirit and is given daily increase by means of the sacraments and the Word of God.

I believe that no one can be saved who is not in this gathering or community, harmoniously sharing the same faith with it, the same word, sacraments, hope, and love, and that no Jew, heretic, pagan, or sinner can be saved along with this community unless they become reconciled with it and unite with it in full agreement in all things.

I believe that in this community or Christendom all things are held in common; what each one possesses belongs also to others, and no one has complete ownership of anything. Hence, all the prayers and good deeds of all the Christian community benefit, aid, and strengthen me and every other believer at all times, both in life and in death, and that each one bears the other's burden, as St. Paul teaches [Gal. 6:2].

I believe that there is forgiveness of sin nowhere else than in this community and that beyond it nothing can help to gain it—no good deeds, no matter how many or how great they might be; and that within this community nothing can invalidate this forgiveness of sin—no matter how gravely and often one may sin; and that such forgiveness continues as long as this one community exists. To this community Christ gave the power of the keys, saying in Matthew 18[:18], "Whatever you bind on earth shall be bound in heaven." He said the same to Peter as an individual, representing and taking the place of the one and only one church, "whatever you bind on earth," and so forth, Matthew 16[:19].

I believe that there will be a resurrection from the dead in the future in which all flesh will be raised from the dead through the Holy Spirit, that is, all humankind, good and evil, will be raised bodily to return alive in the same flesh in which they died, were buried, and decayed or perished in various ways.

I believe in an eternal life for the saints after the resurrection and in an eternal dying for the sinners. And I haven't a doubt about all this that the Father through his Son Jesus Christ our Lord and with the Holy Spirit will let all this happen to me. [This means] Amen, that is, this is [actually and certainly true].

A blessing for when one arises in the morning.
Under the care of God: the Father, Son, and Holy Spirit.

Recite the Creed.
I believe in God the Father almighty, creator, etc.

Pray the Lord's Prayer.
Our Father, you who are in heaven, hallowed be, etc.

Afterward, read something from the Bible and Psalms that may be used to strengthen your faith against all errors, sins, and assaults.

When you go to work
Recite the Ten Commandments and pray an "Our Father," etc.

The [Table] Blessing
Psalm 144 [=104:27-28]

All eyes wait upon you, O LORD, and you give them their food in their season. You open your hand and satisfy every living thing with pleasure. "Our Father," etc.

Prayer

Lord God, heavenly Father, bless us and these your gifts that we receive from your bountiful goodness, through Christ our Lord. Amen.

The Thanksgiving [after Meals]

Give thanks to the Lord, for he is kind, and his goodness endures eternally. He gives food to all flesh. He gives fodder to the cattle, to the young ravens who cry to him. He has no desire for strong horses nor pleasure in anyone's legs. The Lord takes pleasure in those who fear him, who wait for his goodness.

"Our Father."

Prayer

We thank you, Lord God Father, through Jesus Christ our Lord, for all your blessings, you who live and reign in eternity. Amen.

An evening blessing when one goes to bed.
Under the care of God: the Father, Son, and Holy Spirit. Amen.

Psalm 63[:6-7]

When I think of you upon my bed, so was my conversation about you during the [night] watch. For you are my Helper, and under the shadow of your wings I will rejoice.

"Our Father," etc.

And here one must get accustomed to recalling whatever one heard or learned during the day from the Holy Scripture and fall asleep thinking about it.

. . . A Short Exposition of the Lord's Prayer

The Soul: O Our Father, who art in heaven, we your children dwell here on earth in misery, far removed from you. Such a great gulf lies between you and us. How are we to find our way home to you in our fatherland?

God, in Malachi 1[:6]: A child honors its father, and a servant his master. If then I am your Father, where is my honor? If I am your Lord, where is the awe and the reverence due me? For my holy name is blasphemed and dishonored among you and by you, Isaiah 52[:5].

The First Petition [of the Lord's Prayer]

The Soul: My Father, unfortunately that is true. We acknowledge our guilt. Be a merciful Father and do not take us to task, but grant us your grace that your name may be hallowed in us. Let us not think, say, do, have, or undertake anything unless it redounds to your honor and glory. Grant that we may enhance your name and honor it above everything else and that we not seek our own vain glory nor further our own name. Grant that we may love and fear and honor you as children do their father.

God, in Isaiah 52[:5] and Genesis 8[:21]: How can my name and honor be hallowed in you, while your heart and mind are inclined to evil and are captive to sin, and since no one can sing my praise in a foreign land, Psalm 127[:4]?

The Second Petition

The Soul: O Father, that is true. We realize that our members incline to sin and that the world, the flesh, and the devil want to reign in us and thus banish your name and honor from us. Therefore, we ask you to help us out of this misery and to let your kingdom come so that sin may be expelled and we become righteous and acceptable to you, so that you alone may hold sway in us and we may become your kingdom by placing all our powers, both inner and external, in your service.

God in Deuteronomy 32[:39]: Him whom I am to help I destroy. Him whom I want to quicken, save, enrich, and make [righteous], I mortify, reject, impoverish, and reduce to nothing. However, you refuse to accept such counsel and action from me, Psalm 78[:10-11]. How, then, am I to help you? And what more can I do? Isaiah 5[:4].

The Third Petition

The Soul: We deplore that we do not understand or accept your helping hand. O Father, grant us your grace and help us to allow your divine will to be done in us. Yes, even though it pains us, continue to punish and stab us, to beat and burn us. Do as you will with us, as long as your will, and not ours, is done. Dear Father, keep us from undertaking and completing anything that is in accord with our own choice, will, and opinion. [For] your will and ours conflict with each other. Yours alone is good, though it does not seem to be; ours is evil, though it glitters.

God in Psalm 78[:9]: Your lips often voiced your love for me, while your heart was far from me [Isa. 29:13]. And when I chastised you to improve you, you defected; in the midst of my work on you, you deserted me, as you can read in Psalm 78[:9], "They turned back on the day of battle." Those who made a good beginning and moved me to deal with them turned their backs on me and fell back into sin and into my disfavor.

The Fourth Petition

The Soul: O Father, this is very true; "for not by his might shall a man prevail," 1 Samuel 2[:9]. And who can abide under your hand if you yourself do not strengthen and comfort us? Therefore, dear Father, seize hold of us, fulfill your will in us so that we may become your kingdom, to your glory and honor. But, dear Father, fortify us in such trials with your holy Word; give us our daily bread. Fashion your dear Son, Jesus Christ, the true heavenly bread, in our hearts so that we, strengthened by him, may cheerfully bear and endure the destruction and death of our will and the perfecting of your will. Yes, grant grace also to all members of Christendom and send us learned priests and pastors who do not feed us the husk and chaff of vain fables, but who teach us your holy gospel and Jesus Christ.

God, in Jeremiah 5[:5-6] and other passages: It is not good to take what is holy and the children's bread and throw it to the dogs [Matt. 7:6; 15:26]. You sin daily, and when I have my Word preached to you day and night, you do not obey and listen, and my Word is despised [Jer. 5:5-6; Isa. 42:20].

The Fifth Petition

The Soul: O Father, have mercy on us and do not deny us our precious bread because of that. We are sorry that we do not do justice to your holy Word, and we implore you to have patience with us poor children. Take away our guilt and do not enter into judgment with us, for no one is just in your sight. Remember your promise to forgive those who sincerely forgive their debtors. It is not that we merit your forgiveness because we forgive others, but we know that you are truthful and will graciously forgive all who forgive their neighbors. We place our trust in your promise.

God in Psalm 78[:8]: I forgive and redeem you so often, and you do not remain steadfast and faithful. You are of weak faith [Matt. 8:26]. You cannot watch and tarry with me a little while, but quickly fall back into temptation. [Matthew 26:40-41].

The Sixth Petition

The Soul: O Father, we are faint and ill, and the trials in the flesh and in the world are severe and manifold. O dear Father, hold us and do not let us fall into temptation and sin again, but give us grace to remain steadfast and fight valiantly to the end. Without your grace and your help, we are not able to do anything.

God in Psalm 11[:7]: I am just, and my judgment is right. Therefore sin must not go unpunished. Thus you must endure adversity. The fact that trials ensue from this is the fault of your sin, which forces me to punish and curb it.

The Seventh Petition

The Soul: Since trials flow from these adversities and tempt us to sin, deliver us, dear Father, from these so that freed from all sin and adversity according to your divine will we may be your kingdom and laud and praise and hallow you forever. Amen. And since you taught and commanded us to pray thus and have promised fulfillment, we hope and are assured, O dearest Father, that in honor of your truth you will grant all this to us graciously and mercifully.

And finally someone may say, "What am I to do if I cannot believe that I am heard?" Answer: Then follow the example of the father of the child possessed with a dumb spirit in Mark 9[:23-24]. When Christ said to him, "Can you believe? All things are possible to him who believes," the father cried with tear-filled eyes, "O Lord, I believe; help my faith [when] it is too weak!"

Reflection Questions

1. The "Instruction" and the explanation of the Creed follow "The Lay Bible." Why is that important, theologically and as a method of teaching?

2. Why would Luther call "The Lay Bible," "The Lay Bible"?

3. What is the significance of the connection the booklet makes between work and reciting the Ten Commandments, followed by the Lord's Prayer (p. 64)?

4. How does Luther interpret "our daily bread," in the fourth petition of the Lord's Prayer?

5.   In what ways do you find Luther's approach of enhancing prayer life through attention to the Creed, Ten Commandments, and Lord's Prayer helpful? How might you "reorganize" your personal prayer life based on Luther's approach?

3

A Simple Way to Pray (for a Good Friend)

1535

This document represents Luther's mature catechetical piety, the integration of theology and prayer in the context of catechesis. He shows here his long-standing attention to the practical concerns of the Christian life. His response to the question of his barber shows how the reformer viewed this kind of Reformation—believers living at the nexus of the Word of God, catechesis, and prayer. As a confessor of the faith, Luther recommends that believers "pray" the chief articles of the church's confession, that is "the Lay Bible," as found in the catechism.

This classic expression of Luther's reformation priorities went through some twenty-two German editions. The version here is condensed from Luther's Works, *volume 43, pages 188-211.*

≈

How One Should Pray, For Peter, the Master Barber

Dear Master Peter: I offer you as best I can what I do personally when I pray. May our Lord God grant to you and to everyone else the ability to do it better. Amen.

First, when I feel that I have become cold and disinterested in prayer because of various tasks or thoughts (for the flesh and the devil always impede and obstruct prayer), I take my little Book of Psalms, hurry to my room, or, if it be the day and hour for it, to the church where a congregation is assembled. As time permits, I say quietly to myself and word-for-word the Ten Commandments, the Creed, and if I have time, some words of Christ or of Paul, or some psalms, just as children do.

It is a good thing to let prayer be the first business of the morning and the last at night. Guard yourself carefully against those false, deluding ideas which tell you, "Wait a little while. I will pray in an hour. First I must attend to this or that." Such thoughts get you away from prayer into other activities which so hold your attention and involve you that nothing comes of prayer for that day.

It may well be that you may have some tasks which are as good as or better than prayer, especially in an emergency. There is a saying ascribed to St. Jerome: "Everything a believer does is prayer." And there is the proverb, "The one who works faithfully prays twice." This can be said because believers fear and honor God in their work and remember the commandment not to wrong anyone, or to try to steal, defraud, or cheat. Such thoughts and such faith undoubtedly transform their work into prayer and a sacrifice of praise.

However, it is also true that a work done without faith is an outright curse—and so whoever works faithlessly, curses twice. While such people strive, their thoughts are occupied with a neglect of God and violation of Divine law—how to take advantage of neighbors, how to steal from them and defraud them. What else can such thoughts be but out and out curses against God and humankind? They make such work and effort a double curse, by which people curse themselves. In the end, they are beggars and bunglers. It is of such continual prayer that Christ says in Luke 11, "Pray without ceasing," because one must unceasingly guard against sin and wrong-doing, something one cannot do unless one fears God and keeps the divine commandment in mind, as Psalm 1 [:1, 2] says, "Blessed is he who meditates upon his law day and night."

Yet we must be careful not to break the habit of true prayer and imagine other works to be necessary, which after all, are nothing of the kind. Thus at the end we become lax and lazy, cool and listless toward prayer. The devil that oppresses us is not lazy or careless, and our flesh is too ready and eager to sin and is disinclined to the spirit of prayer.

When your heart has been warmed by such recitation to yourself [of the Ten Commandments, the words of Christ, etc.] and is intent upon the matter, kneel or stand with your hands folded and your eyes toward heaven and speak or think as briefly as you can:

"O Heavenly Father, dear God, I am a poor unworthy sinner. I do not deserve to raise my eyes or hands toward you or to pray. But because you have commanded us all to pray and have promised to hear us and through your dear Son Jesus Christ have taught us both how and what to pray, I come to you in obedience to your word, trusting in your gracious promise. I pray in the name of my Lord Jesus Christ together with all your saints and Christians on earth as he has taught us: Our Father in Heaven, etc., through the whole prayer, word-for-word."

Then repeat one part or as much as you wish, perhaps the first petition: "Hallowed be your name." Say, "Yes, Lord God, dear Father, hallowed be your name, both in us and throughout the whole world. Destroy and root out the abominations, idolatry, and heresy of the Turk, the pope, and all false teachers and fanatics who wrongly use your name and in scandalous ways take it in vain and horribly blaspheme it. They incessantly boast that they teach your word and the laws of the church. However, they really use the devil's deceit and trickery in your name wretchedly to seduce many poor souls throughout the world, even killing and shedding much innocent blood. In such persecution, they believe that they render you a divine service.

"Dear Lord God, convert and restrain [them]. Convert those who are still to be converted that they with us and we with them may hallow and praise your name, both with true and pure doctrine and with a good and holy life. Restrain those who are unwilling to be converted so that they are forced to cease from misusing, defiling, and dishonoring your holy name and from misleading the poor people. Amen."

The second petition: "Your kingdom come." Say: "O dear Lord, God and Father, you see how worldly wisdom and reason not only profane your name and ascribe the honor due to you to lies and to the devil. They also take the power, might, wealth, and glory that you have given them on earth for ruling the world and thus serving you, and use it in their own ambition to oppose your kingdom. They are many and mighty. They plague and hinder the tiny flock of your kingdom who are weak, despised, and few. They will not tolerate your flock on earth and think that by plaguing them they render a great and godly service to you. Dear Lord, God and Father, convert them and defend us. Convert those who are still to become children and members of your kingdom so that they with us and we with them may serve you in your kingdom in true faith and unfeigned love and that from your kingdom which has begun, we may enter into your eternal kingdom. Defend us against those who will not turn away their might and power from the destruction of your kingdom so that when they are cast down from their thrones and humbled, they will have to cease from their efforts. Amen."

The third petition: "Your will be done on earth as it is in heaven." Say: "O dear Lord, God and Father, you know that the world, if it cannot destroy your name or root out your kingdom, is busy day and night. It seeks to destroy your name, word, kingdom, and children with wicked tricks and schemes, strange conspiracies and intrigue. The world huddles together in secret counsel, giving mutual encouragement and support, raging and threatening and going about with every evil intention to destroy your name. Therefore, dear Lord, God and Father, convert them and defend us. Convert those who have yet to acknowledge your good will that they with us and we with them may obey your will and for your sake gladly, patiently, and joyously bear every evil, cross, and adversity, and thereby acknowledge, test, and experience your benign, gracious, and perfect will. But defend us against those who in their rage, fury, hate, threats, and evil desires do not cease to do us harm. Make their wicked schemes, tricks, and devices to come to nothing so that these may be turned against them, as we sing in Psalm 7 [: 16]" . . .

Finally, mark this, that you must always speak the "Amen" firmly. Never doubt that God in his mercy will surely hear you and say "yes" to your prayers. Never think that you are kneeling or standing alone. Rather think that the whole of Christendom, all devout Christians, are standing there beside you and you are standing among them in a common, united petition that God cannot disdain. Do not leave your prayer without having said or thought, "Very well, God has heard my prayer; this I know as a certainty and a truth." That is what Amen means.

You should also know that I do not want you to recite all these words in your prayer. That would make it nothing but idle chatter and babble, read word-for-word out of a book (as were the rosaries by the laity and the prayers of the priests and monks). I want your heart to be stirred and guided concerning the thoughts that ought to be comprehended in the Lord's Prayer. These thoughts may be expressed, if your heart is rightly warmed and inclined toward prayer, in many different ways and with more words or fewer. I do not bind myself to such words or syllables, but say my prayers in one fashion today, in another tomorrow, depending upon my mood and feeling. I stay however, as nearly as I can, with the same general thoughts and ideas. It may happen occasionally that I may get lost among so many ideas in one petition that I pass on the other six. If such an abundance of good thoughts comes to us we ought to disregard the other petitions, make room for such thoughts, listen in silence, and under no circumstances obstruct them. The Holy Spirit preaches here, and one word of the Spirit's sermon is far better than a thousand of our prayers. Many times I have learned more from one prayer than I might have learned from much reading and speculation.

It is of great importance that the heart be made ready and eager for prayer. As the Preacher says, "Prepare your heart for prayer, and do not tempt God" [Ecclus. 18:23]. What else is it but tempting God when your mouth babbles and the mind wanders to other thoughts? Like the priest who prayed: "Make haste, O God, to deliver me (Ps. 70:1)—Farmhand, did you unhitch the horses? Make haste to help me, O Lord—Maid, go out and milk the cow. Glory be to the Father and to the Son and to the Holy Ghost.—Hurry up, boy, I wish the fever would take you!"

I have heard many such prayers in my experience under the papacy; most of their prayers are of this sort. This is blasphemy and it would be better if they played at it if they cannot or do not care to do better. In my day I have prayed many such canonical hours myself, regrettably, and in such a manner that the psalm or the allotted time came to an end before I even realized whether I was at the beginning or in the middle.

Though not all of them blurt out the words as did the above-mentioned cleric and mix business and prayer, they do it by the thoughts in their hearts. They jump from one thing to another in their thoughts and when it is all over they do not know what they have done or what they talked about. They start with Praise and right away they are in a fool's paradise. It seems to me that if someone could see what arises as prayer from a cold and inattentive heart he would conclude that he had never seen a more ridiculous kind of buffoonery. But, praise God, it is now clear to me that a person who forgets what he has said has not prayed well. In a good prayer one fully remembers every word and thought from the beginning to the end of the prayer.

So, a good and attentive barber keeps his thoughts, attention, and eyes on the razor and hair and does not forget how far he has gotten with his shaving or cutting. If he wants to engage in too much conversation or let his mind wander or look somewhere else he is likely to cut his customer's mouth, nose, or even his throat. Thus if anything is to be done well, it requires the full attention of all one's senses and members, as the proverb says, "The one who thinks of many things, thinks of nothing and does nothing right." How much more does prayer call for concentration and singleness of heart if it is to be a good prayer?

To this day, I suckle at the Lord's Prayer like a child. As an old man, I eat and drink from it and never get my fill. It is the very best prayer, even better than the Psalms, which is so very dear to me. It is surely evident that a real master composed and taught it. What a great pity that the prayer of such a master is prattled and blathered so irreverently all over the world! How many pray the Lord's Prayer several thousand times in the course of a year? Moreover, if they were to keep on doing so for a thousand years they would not have tasted nor prayed one iota, one dot, of it! In a word, the Lord's Prayer is the greatest martyr on earth (as are the name and word of God).

If I have had time and opportunity to go through the Lord's Prayer, I do the same with the Ten Commandments. I take one part after another and free myself as much as possible from distractions in order to pray. I divide each commandment into four parts, as I form a garland of four strands. That is, I think of each commandment as, first, instruction, which is really what it is intended to be, and consider what the Lord God demands of me so earnestly. Second, I turn it into a thanksgiving; third, a confession; and fourth, a prayer. I do so in thoughts or words such as these:

"I am the Lord your God, etc. You shall have no other gods before me," etc. First, I consider what God expects from me and teaches me: I am expected to trust wholeheartedly in all circumstances that God sincerely intends to be my God. I must think of God in this way at the risk of losing eternal salvation. My heart must not build upon anything else or trust in any other thing, be it wealth, prestige, wisdom, might, piety, or anything else. Second, I give thanks for his infinite compassion by which he has come to me in such a fatherly way and, unasked, unbidden, and unmerited, has offered to be my God, to care for me, and to be my comfort, guardian, help, and strength in every time of need. We poor mortals have sought so many gods and would have to seek them still if he did not enable us to hear him openly tell us in our own language that he intends to be our God. How could we ever—in all eternity—thank God enough! Third, I confess and acknowledge my great sin and ingratitude for having so shamefully despised such sublime teachings and such a precious gift throughout my whole life, and for having fearfully provoked his wrath by countless acts of idolatry. I repent of these and ask for his grace. Fourth, I pray and say: "O my God and Lord, help me by your grace to learn and understand your commandments more fully every day and to live by them in sincere confidence. Preserve my heart so that I shall never again become forgetful and ungrateful, that I may never seek after other gods or other consolation on earth or in any creature, but cling truly and solely to you, my only God. Amen, dear Lord God and Father. Amen."

Afterward, if time and inclination permit, I pray the Second Commandment likewise in four strands, like this: "You shall not take the name of the Lord your God in vain," etc. First, I learn that I must keep God's name in honor, holiness, and beauty; not to swear, curse, not to be boastful or seek honor and repute for myself, but humbly to invoke his name, to pray, praise, and extol it, and to let it be my only honor and glory that he is my God and that I am his lowly creature and unworthy servant. Second, I give thanks to him for these precious gifts, that he has revealed his name to me and bestowed it upon me, that I can glory in his name and be called God's servant and creature, etc., that his name is my refuge like a mighty fortress to which the righteous man can flee and find protection, as Solomon says [Proverbs 18:10]. Third, I confess and acknowledge that I have grievously and shamefully sinned against this commandment all my life. I have not only failed to invoke, extol, and honor his holy name, but have also been ungrateful for such gifts and have, by swearing, lying, and betraying, misused them in the pursuit of shame and sin. This I bitterly regret and ask grace and forgiveness, etc. Fourth, I ask for help and strength henceforth to learn [to obey] this command-ment and to be preserved from such evil ingratitude, abuse, and sin against his name, and that I may be found grateful in revering and honoring his name.

I repeat here what I previously said in reference to the Lord's Prayer: if in the midst of such thoughts the Holy Spirit begins to preach in your heart with rich, enlightening thoughts, honor him by letting go of this written scheme. Be still and listen to the one who can do better than you can. Remember what the Spirit says and note it well and you will behold wondrous things in the law of God, as David says [Ps. 119:18].

The Third Commandment: "Remember the Sabbath day, to keep it holy." I learn from this, first of all, that the Sabbath day has not been instituted for the sake of being idle or indulging in worldly pleasures, but in order that we may keep it holy. However, it is not sanctified by our works and actions, but by the word of God. Our works are not holy. The word of God alone is totally pure and sacred. It sanctifies everything that comes in contact with it—time, place, person, labor, rest, etc. According to St. Paul, who says that every creature is consecrated by word and prayer, I Timothy 4 [:5], our works are consecrated through the word. I realize therefore that on the Sabbath I must, above all, hear and contemplate God's word. Thereafter I should give thanks in my own words, praise God for all his benefits, and pray for myself and for the whole world. The one who does this on the Sabbath keeps it holy. The one who fails to do so is worse than the person who works on the Sabbath.

Second, I thank God in this commandment for the great and beautiful divine goodness and grace which has been given to us in the preaching of God's word. And God has instructed us to make use of it, especially on the Sabbath day, for the meditation of the human heart can never exhaust such a treasure. The word of God is the only light in the darkness of this life, a word of life, consolation, and supreme blessedness. Where this precious and saving word is absent, nothing remains but a fearsome and terrifying darkness, error and faction, death and every calamity, and the tyranny of the devil himself, as we can see with our own eyes every day.

Third, I confess and acknowledge great sin and wicked ingratitude on my part because all my life I have made disgraceful use of the Sabbath and have thereby despised God's precious and dear word in a wretched way. I have been too lazy, listless, and uninterested to listen to it, let alone to have desired it sincerely or to have been grateful for it. I have let my dear God proclaim the word to me in vain, have dismissed the noble treasure, and have trampled it underfoot. God has tolerated this with great and divine mercy and has not ceased in his fatherly, divine love and faithfulness to keep on preaching to me and calling me to the salvation of my soul. For this I repent and ask for grace and forgiveness.

Fourth, I pray for myself and for the whole world that the gracious Father may preserve us in his holy word and not withdraw it from us because of our sin, ingratitude, and laziness. May God preserve us from factious spirits and false teachers. May God send faithful and honest laborers into the harvest [Matt. 9:38], that is, devout pastors and preachers. May God grant us grace humbly to hear, accept, and honor their words as the word of God and to offer our sincere thanks and praise.

The Fourth Commandment: "Honor your father and your mother." First, I learn to acknowledge God, my Creator; how wondrously God has created me, body and soul; and has given me life through my parents and has instilled in them the desire to care for me, the fruit of their bodies, with all their power. He has brought me into this world, has sustained and cared for me, nurtured and educated me with great diligence, carefulness, and concern, through danger, trouble, and hard work. To this moment he protects me, his creature, and helps me in countless dangers and troubles. It is as though he were creating me anew every moment. But the devil does not willingly concede us one single moment of life.

Second, I thank the rich and gracious Creator on behalf of myself and all the world that he has established and assured in the commandment the increase and preservation of the human race, that is, of households and of states. Without these two institutions or governments the world could not exist a single year, because without government there can be no peace, and where there is no peace there can be no family; without family, children cannot be begotten or raised, and fatherhood and motherhood would cease to be. It is the purpose of this commandment to guard and preserve both family and state, to admonish children and subjects to be obedient, and to enforce it, too, and to let no violation go unpunished. Otherwise, children would have disrupted the family long ago by their disobedience, and subjects would have disorganized the state and laid it to waste, because they outnumber parents and rulers. There are no words fully to describe the benefit of this commandment.

Third, I confess and lament my wicked disobedience and sin; in defiance of God's commandment I have not honored or obeyed my parents; I have often provoked and offended them, have been impatient with their parental discipline, have been resentful and scornful of their loving admonition and have rather gone along with loose company and evil companions. God himself condemns such disobedient children and withholds from them a long life; many of them succumb and perish in disgrace before they reach adulthood. Whoever does not obey father and mother must obey the executioner or otherwise come, through God's wrath, to an evil end, etc. Of all this I repent and ask for grace and forgiveness.

Fourth, I pray for myself and for the entire world—that God would bestow his grace and pour his blessing richly upon the family and the state. Grant that from this time on we may be devout, honor our parents, obey our superiors, and resist the devil when he entices us to be disobedient and rebellious. Thus, we may we help improve home and nation by our actions and thus preserve the peace, all to the praise and glory of God for our own benefit and for the prosperity of all. Grant that we may acknowledge these his gifts and be thankful for them.

At this point, we should add a prayer for our parents and superiors, that God may grant them understanding and wisdom to govern and rule us in peace and happiness. May God preserve them from tyranny, from riot and fury, and turn them to honor the divine Word and not oppress it, nor persecute anyone or do injustice. Prayer must seek such excellent gifts, as St. Paul teaches; otherwise the devil will reign in the palace and everything fall into chaos and confusion.

If you are a father or mother, you should at this point remember your children and the workers in your household. Pray earnestly to the dear Father, who has set you in an office of honor in his name and intends that the name "father" or "mother," honor you. Ask that he grant you grace and blessing to look after and support your wife, children, and servants in a godly and Christian manner. May he give you wisdom and strength to train them well in heart and will to follow your instruction with obedience. Both are God's gifts, your children and the way they flourish, that they turn out well and that they remain so. Otherwise, the home is nothing but a pigsty and school for rascals, as one can see among the uncouth and godless.

The Fifth Commandment: "You shall not kill." Here I learn, first of all, that God desires me to love my neighbor, so that I do him no bodily harm, either by word or action, neither injure nor take revenge upon him in anger, vexation, envy, hatred, or for any evil reason, but realize that I am obliged to assist and counsel him in every bodily need. In this commandment, God commands me to protect my neighbor's body and in turn commands my neighbor to protect my own. As Sirach says, "He has committed to each of us his neighbor" [Ecclus. 9:14].

Second, I give thanks for such ineffable love, providence, and faithfulness toward me by which he has placed this mighty shield and wall to protect my physical safety. All are obliged to care for me and protect me, and I, in turn, must behave likewise toward others. He upholds this command and, where it is not observed, he has established the sword as punishment for those who do not live up to it. Were it not for this excellent commandment and ordinance, the devil would instigate such a massacre among men that no one could live in safety for a single hour—as happens when God becomes angry and inflicts punishment upon a disobedient and ungrateful world.

Third, I confess and lament my own wickedness and that of the world. Not only are we so terribly ungrateful for such fatherly love and solicitude toward us, what is especially scandalous, is that we do not acknowledge this commandment and teaching. We are unwilling to learn it. We neglect it as though it did not concern us or we had no part in it. We amble along complacently, feeling no remorse that in defiance of this commandment, we neglect our neighbors, and, yes, we desert them, persecute, injure, or even kill them in our thoughts. We indulge in anger, rage, and villainy as though we were doing a fine and noble thing. Really, it is high time that we started to deplore and bewail how much we have acted like rogues and like unseeing, unruly, and unfeeling persons who kick, scratch, tear, and devour one another like furious beasts and pay no heed to this serious and divine command, etc.

Fourth, I pray the dear Father to lead us to an understanding of this his sacred commandment and to help us keep it and live in accordance with it. May he preserve us from the murderer who is the master of every form of murder and violence. May he grant us his grace that we and all others may treat each other in kindly, gentle, charitable ways, forgiving one another from the heart, bearing each other's faults and shortcomings in a Christian and brotherly manner, and thus living together in true peace and concord, as the commandment teaches and requires us to do.

The Sixth Commandment: "You shall not commit adultery." Here I learn once again, what God intends and expects me to do, namely, to live chastely, decently, and temperately, both in thoughts and in words and actions, and not to disgrace any one's spouse, child, or servant. More than this, I ought to assist, save, protect, and guard marriage and decency to the best of my ability. I should silence the idle thoughts of those who want to destroy and slander their reputation. All this I am obliged to do, and God expects me not only to leave my neighbor's spouse and family unmolested, but I owe it to my neighbors to preserve and protect their good character and honor, just as I would want my neighbors to do for me and mine in keeping with this commandment.

Second, I thank my faithful and dear Father for his grace and benevolence by which he accepts my husband, son, servant, wife, daughter, maidservant into his care and protection and forbids so sternly and firmly anything, that would bring them into disrepute. God protects and upholds this commandment and does not leave violations unpunished, even though he himself has to act if someone disregards and violates the commandment and precept. No one escapes. They must either pay the penalty or eventually atone for such lust in the fires of hell. God desires chastity; God will not tolerate adultery. We can see that every day, when God's wrath overtakes the impenitent and profligate and they perish miserably. Otherwise, it would be impossible to guard one's spouse, child, and servants against the devil's filthiness for a single hour or preserve them in honor and decency. What would happen would be unbridled immorality and beastliness, as happens when God in his wrath withdraws his hand and permits everything to go to wrack and ruin.

Third, I confess and acknowledge my sin, my own and that of all the world, how I have sinned against this commandment my whole life in thought, word, and action. Not only have I been ungrateful for these excellent teachings and gifts, but I have complained and rebelled against the divine requirement of such decency and chastity, that God has not permitted all sorts of fornication and rascality to go unchecked and unpunished. He will not allow marriage to be despised, ridiculed, or condemned, etc. Sins against this commandment are, above all others, the grossest and most conspicuous and cannot be covered up or whitewashed. For this I am sorry, etc.

Fourth, I pray for myself and all the world that God may grant us grace to keep this commandment gladly and cheerfully in order that we might ourselves live in chastity and also help and support others to do likewise.

Then I continue with the other commandments as I have time or opportunity or am in the mood for it. As I have said before, I do not want anyone to feel bound by my words or thoughts. I only want to offer an example for those who may wish to follow it; let anyone improve it who is able to do so and let him meditate either upon all commandments at one time or on as many as he may desire. For the mind, once it is seriously occupied with a matter, be it good or evil, can ponder more in one moment than the tongue can recite in ten hours or the pen write in ten days. There is something quick, subtle, and mighty about the mind and soul. It is able to review the Ten Commandments in their fourfold aspect very rapidly if it wants to do so and is in earnest.

The Seventh Commandment: "You shall not steal." First, I can learn here that I must not take my neighbor's property from him or possess it against his will, either in secret or openly. I must not be false or dishonest in business, service, or work, nor profit by fraud, but must support myself by the sweat of my brow and eat my bread in honor. Furthermore, I must see to it that in any of the above-named ways my neighbor is not defrauded, just as I wish for myself. I also learn in this commandment that God, in his fatherly solicitude, sets a protective hedge around my goods and solemnly prohibits anyone to steal from me. Where that is ignored, he has imposed a penalty and has placed the gallows and the rope in the hands of Jack the hangman. Where that cannot be done, God himself metes out punishment and they become beggars in the end, as the proverb says, "Who steals in his youth, goes begging in old age," or, "Stolen gain goes down the drain."

In addition, I give thanks for his steadfast goodness in that he has given such excellent teachings, assurance, and protection to me and to the entire world. If it were not for his protection, not a penny or a crumb of bread would be left in the house.

Third, I confess my sins and ingratitude in such instances where I have wronged, deprived, or cheated anyone in my life.

Fourth, I ask that he grant grace to me and the entire world, so that we might learn from this commandment, ponder it, and become better people. Thus, there may be less theft, robbery, usury, cheating, and injustice and that the Judgment Day, for which all saints and the whole creation pray, Romans 8 [:20–23], shall soon end this. Amen.

The Eighth Commandment: "You shall not bear false witness." This teaches us, first of all, to be truthful to each other, to shun lies and calumnies, to be glad to speak well of each other, and to delight in hearing what is good about others. Thus a wall has been built around our good reputation and integrity to protect it against malicious gossip and deceitful tongues; God will not let that go unpunished, as he has said in the other commandments.

We owe God thanks, both for the teachings and the protection that have so graciously been provided for us.

Third, we confess and ask forgiveness that we have spent our lives in ingratitude and sin and have maligned our neighbors with false and wicked talk, though we owe them the same preservation of honor and integrity that we desire for ourselves.

Fourth, we ask for help from now on to keep the commandment and for a healing tongue, etc.

The Ninth and Tenth Commandments: "You shall not covet your neighbor's house." Similarly, "his wife," etc.

This teaches us first that we shall not dispossess our neighbors of their goods under pretense of legal claims, or lure away, alienate, or extort what is theirs. Rather, we should help them keep what is theirs, just as we wish to be done for ourselves. This is also a protection against the subtleties and chicaneries of shrewd manipulators, who will receive their punishment in the end. Second, we should render thanks to God. Third, we should repentantly and sorrowfully confess our sins. Fourth, we should ask for help and strength devoutly to keep such divine commandments.

These are the Ten Commandments in their fourfold aspect, namely, as a school text, songbook, penitential book, and prayer book. They are intended to help the heart come to itself and grow zealous in prayer. Take care, however, not to undertake all of this or so much that one becomes weary in spirit. Likewise, a good prayer should not be lengthy or drawn out, but frequent and ardent. It is enough to consider one section or half a section, which kindles a fire in the heart. This the Spirit will grant us and continually instruct us in when, by God's word, our hearts have been cleared and freed of outside thoughts and concerns.

Nothing can be said here about the part of faith and Holy Scriptures [in prayer], because there would be no end to what could be said. With practice, one can take the Ten Commandments on one day, a psalm or chapter of Holy Scripture the next day, and use them as flint and steel to kindle a flame in the heart.

A Simple Exercise for Contemplating the Creed
If you have more time, or the inclination, you may treat the Creed in the same manner and make it into a garland of four strands. The Creed, however, consists of three main parts or articles, corresponding to the three Persons of the Divine Majesty, as it has been so divided in the Catechism and elsewhere.

The First Article of Creation
"I believe in God the Father Almighty, maker of heaven and earth."

Here, first of all, a great light shines into your heart if you permit it to and teaches you in a few words what all the languages of the world and a multitude of books cannot describe or fathom in words, namely, who you are, whence you came, whence came heaven and earth. You are God's creation, God's handiwork, the work of God's hands. That is, of your and in yourself you are nothing, can do nothing, know nothing, are capable of nothing. What were you a thousand years ago? What were heaven and earth six thousand years ago? Nothing, just as that which will never be created is nothing. But what you are, know, can do, and can achieve is God's creation, as you confess [in the Creed] by word of mouth. Therefore you have nothing to boast of before God except that you are nothing and he is your Creator who can annihilate you at any moment. Reason knows nothing of such a light. Many great people have sought to know what heaven and earth, man and creatures are and have found no answer. But here it is declared and faith affirms that God has created everything out of nothing. Here is the soul's garden of pleasure, along whose paths we enjoy the works of God—but it would take too long to describe all that.

Furthermore, we should give thanks to God that in his kindness he has created us out of nothing and provides for our daily needs out of nothing—has made us to be such excellent beings with body and soul, intelligence, five senses, and has ordained us to be masters of earth, of fish, bird, and beast, etc. Here consider Genesis, chapters one to three.

Third, we should confess and lament our lack of faith and gratitude in failing to take this to heart, or to believe, ponder, and acknowledge it, and having been more stupid than unthinking beasts.

Fourth, we pray for a true and confident faith that sincerely esteems and trusts God to be our Creator, as this article declares.

The Second Article of Redemption
"And in Jesus Christ, his only Son, our Lord," etc.

Again, a great light shines forth and teaches us how Christ, God's Son, has redeemed us from death which, after the creation, had become our lot through Adam's fall and in which we would have perished eternally. Now think: just as in the first article you were to consider yourself one of God's creatures and not doubt it, now you must think of yourself as one of the redeemed and never doubt that. Among all the words here, emphasize two words above all others: "for us." Jesus Christ is Lord, for us. Christ suffered for us, died for us, and rose for us. All this is ours and pertains to us. This "us" includes you, as the word of God declares.

Second, you must be sincerely grateful for such grace and rejoice in your salvation.

Third, you must sorrowfully lament and confess your wicked unbelief and mistrust of such a gift. Oh, what thoughts will come to mind—the idolatry you have practiced repeatedly, how much you have made of praying to the saints and of innumerable good works of yours which have opposed such salvation.

Fourth, pray now that God will preserve you from this time forward to the end in true and pure faith in Christ our Lord.

The Third Article of Sanctification
"I believe in the Holy Spirit," etc.

This is the third great light which teaches us where such a Creator and Redeemer may be found and plainly encountered in this world, and what this will all come to in the end. Much could be said about this, but here is a summary: Where the holy Christian church exists, there we can find God the Creator, God the Redeemer, God the Holy Spirit, that is, the One who daily sanctifies us through the forgiveness of sins, etc. The church exists where the word of God concerning such faith is rightly preached and confessed.

Again, you have occasion here to ponder long about everything that the Holy Spirit accomplishes in the church every day, etc.

Therefore, be thankful that you have been called and have come into such a church.

Confess and lament your lack of faith and gratitude, that you have neglected all this, and pray for a true and steadfast faith that will remain and endure until you come to that place where all endures forever, that is, beyond the resurrection from the dead, in life eternal. Amen.

Reflection Questions

1. If Luther is right that "the one who works faithfully prays twice," then what would that mean for the way you live your everyday life—at your job, in your family, with friends and neighbors, etc.?

2. In what ways do the educational programs at your church focus on teaching students, young and old alike, to pray?

3. What interferes with your ability to pray?

4. How might Luther's practice of prayer (with its catechism-based "garland" of instruction, thanksgiving, confession, and prayer) deepen the times you spend in conscious, structured prayer?

5. Based on all you've read in this book, what "advice on prayer" would you offer to others—be they children, friends, neighbors, etc.?

Conclusion

There is a saying in church circles: "If you want to see if God has a sense humor, make plans." The implication, of course, is that God leads believers in ways they cannot always anticipate. Martin Luther's life seems to bear this out—the "thorough reformation" he thought he did "not have the time to undertake" when he wrote the cover letter to the Personal Prayer Book *in 1522, was to become the reformer's life's work. Luther himself seemed to be aware of this irony when, years later, he sat at table and looked back on how God "drew" him to emphasize the reformation of the church's theology and practice of prayer:*

> When I was a monk I was unwilling to omit any of the prayers, but when I was busy with public lecturing and writing I often accumulated my appointed prayers for the whole week, or even two or three weeks. Then I would take a Saturday off, or shut myself in for as long as three days without food and drink, until I had said the prescribed prayers. This made my head split, and as a consequence I couldn't close my eyes for five nights, lay sick unto death, and went out of my senses. Even after I had quickly recovered and I tried again to read, my head went 'round and 'round. Thus our Lord God drew me, as if by force, from that torment of prayers. . . .

~

The experience of prayer Luther describes here stands in stark contrast to how he experienced prayer later in his life. The move is dramatic. His own prayer life went from "torment" to the warm, realistic, and life-giving practice of prayer, about which Luther was to teach and preach so eloquently later. This shift indicates the core of Luther's reformation career. In addition, this shift indicates how he became so intensely interested in praying for reform.

In Luther's life and work, prayer and theology are inseparable—prayer implies theology and theology implies prayer. In many ways, Luther's theology itself is a sort of prayer. This is why the reformer would list prayer as a distinctive feature of the Christian community. In *On the Councils and the Church* (1539), he calls prayer a "mark" or "sign" of the church. From Luther's perspective, the Protestant Reformation included a reformation of prayer. This led him to call for a reformation of how the church understood itself in relationship to God—as well as a reformation of how the church understood God's involvement with the church and world. A reformation of Christian prayer is in many ways what Luther intended as a practical outcome of his attempts to reform the church. That is why if we would understand Martin Luther, then we would do well to understand why and how he spent his life praying for reform.

Postscript for Lutherans

"To this day, I nurse at the Lord's Prayer like a child, and as an old man eat and drink from it and never get my fill." (*Simple Way to Pray [for a Good Friend]*)

"But this I say for myself . . . I must still read and study the catechism daily, and yet I cannot master it as I wish, but must remain a child and pupil of the catechism—and I also do so gladly." (Preface to the *Large Catechism)*

∾

As we move into the 21st century, Luther's radical call to a life of study and prayer has never been more important for Lutherans to hear. In our age of technology and globalization, when "World Christianity" is right outside our doors and non-Christians are our neighbors, we need to know who we are. We need to understand the distinctiveness of our identity and mission as Lutheran Christians.

If Luther is right, this identity and mission flow out of attention to the catechism. More precisely, they flow out of studying the Word of God from the perspective of the catechism. The catechism functions as the interpretive tool for the life-long study of God's Word. This "catechetical hermeneutic" is not the only perspective in the church catholic. It is, however, ours. It is incumbent upon us to appreciate and live from the standpoint of the catechism—with its emphasis on prayer founded on justification by faith alone. It is our calling as Lutherans to teach and preach self-consciously from this perspective.

While we study the catechism, Luther would also have us pray—daily. This kind of prayer embraces our entire lives. As forgiven sinners and beloved children of God, we live together in the relationship that God has established with us in Jesus Christ. We pray intentionally—meditating on the catechism and the Scriptures as we learn, give thanks, confess our failings, and pray for strength to live faithful lives. We begin and end our days in conscious contact with God.

Moreover, Luther calls us to pray with our lives. We enter the world every day with the Word on our lips—contemplating what God has done for us and considering what it is that God calls us to do. In other words, we seek to live our vocations as Christians in the world—working diligently and honestly to serve others in the communities where we work and play, and in the world.

At the end of the day, this is Luther's legacy: study of the Word and prayer in the name of the Word made flesh. This is what it means to pray for reform in our day. This is what endures. This is what makes it important to know about Luther, prayer, and the Christian life.

Select Bibliography

_____*That I Might Be His Own: An Overview of Luther's Catechisms* (St. Louis: Concordia Publishing House, 2000).

John Doberstein, *Minister's Prayer Book* (Muhlenberg Press: Philadelphia, 1959). This was reprinted in 1986, by Fortress Press.

George W. Forell, *Faith Active in Love* (Minneapolis: Augsburg, 1954).

John W. Kleinig, "The Kindred Heart: Luther on Meditation," in *The Lutheran Theological Journal,* v. 20, number 243, 1986, 142ff.

Robert Kolb and Timothy Wengert, eds., *The Book of Concord* (Fortress Press: Minneapolis, 2000).

_____and James Nestingen, eds., *Sources and Contexts of the Book of Concord* (Fortress Press, 2001).

Gottfried Krodel, "Luther's Work in the Catechism in the Context of Late Medieval Catechetical Literature," in *Concordia Journal,* volume 25, October 1999.

Martin Luther, "Exposition of the Lord's Prayer for Simple Laymen," in *Luther's Works,* volume 42, 15ff.

William R. Russell, *Luther's Theological Testament: The Schmalkald Articles* (St. Louis: Concordia Publishing House, forthcoming in 2006).

Martha Ellen Stortz, "Practicing Christians," in *The Promise of Lutheran Ethics,* ed. by Karen Bloomquist and John Stumme (Fortress Press: Minneapolis), 1998, 55ff.

John Thornton and Susan Varenne, eds., *Faith and Freedom: An Invitation to the Writings of Martin Luther* (New York: Vintage Spiritual Classics, 2002).

Marjorie Thompson, *A Simple Way to Pray by Martin Luther* (Westminster John Knox, 2000).

C. J. Trapp, *Martin Luther's A Simple Way to Pray* (Milwaukee: Northwestern Pub. House, 1983).

Timothy Wengert, "Wittenberg's Earliest Catechism," *Lutheran Quarterly,* n.s., 7 (1993): 247-260.